Jananne Al-Ani

Film and Video Umbrella

Foreword | Steven Bode

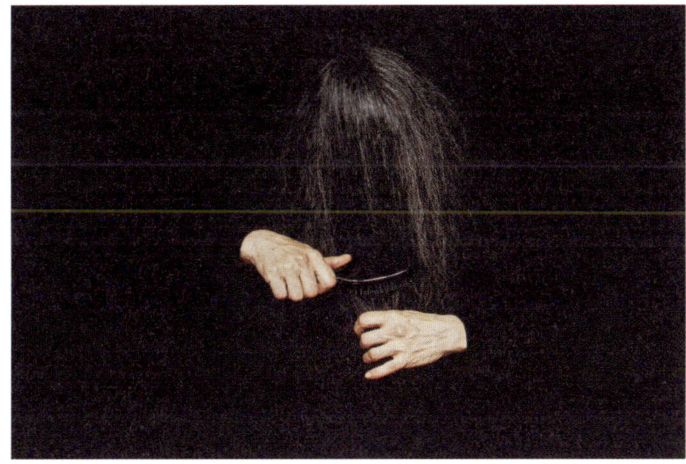

In many of Jananne Al-Ani's photographic and video works a veil exists between the viewer and the subject. In some, that veil is tangible and literal — women's faces partly shadowed by folds of fabric, or completely hidden behind a mop of hair. In others, it is optical, perceptual — a shimmer of heat haze in a desert, a cloud of steam in a bathhouse. In others still, it is abstract, metaphorical — a web of words formed from whispered exchanges, eventually growing, through repeated twists and turns, into a cat's cradle of complex meanings.

A formal device that recurs in much of her work, this tendency to simultaneously disguise and disclose is echoed across the many layers of her practice. In several of her pieces, Al-Ani employs members of her immediate family (usually her mother and sisters) as performers, permitting occasional glimpses of personal and family history, but all within a carefully composed theatrical setting that accentuates the universal, almost archetypal nature of the individual stories and relationships. Although nothing very much is ever given away, the intimacy of each scene is both disarming and haunting, leaving the stark, spare beauty of Al-Ani's imagery to imprint itself indelibly on the mind.

This is the first dedicated survey of Jananne Al-Ani's work, highlighting a number of video installations and a selection of photographic pieces dating from 1991 onwards. With the aid of two specially commissioned essays, as well as a long interview with the artist, this book traces themes and preoccupations that have persisted over that time and which continue to reverberate throughout this highly inventive and distinctive body of work.

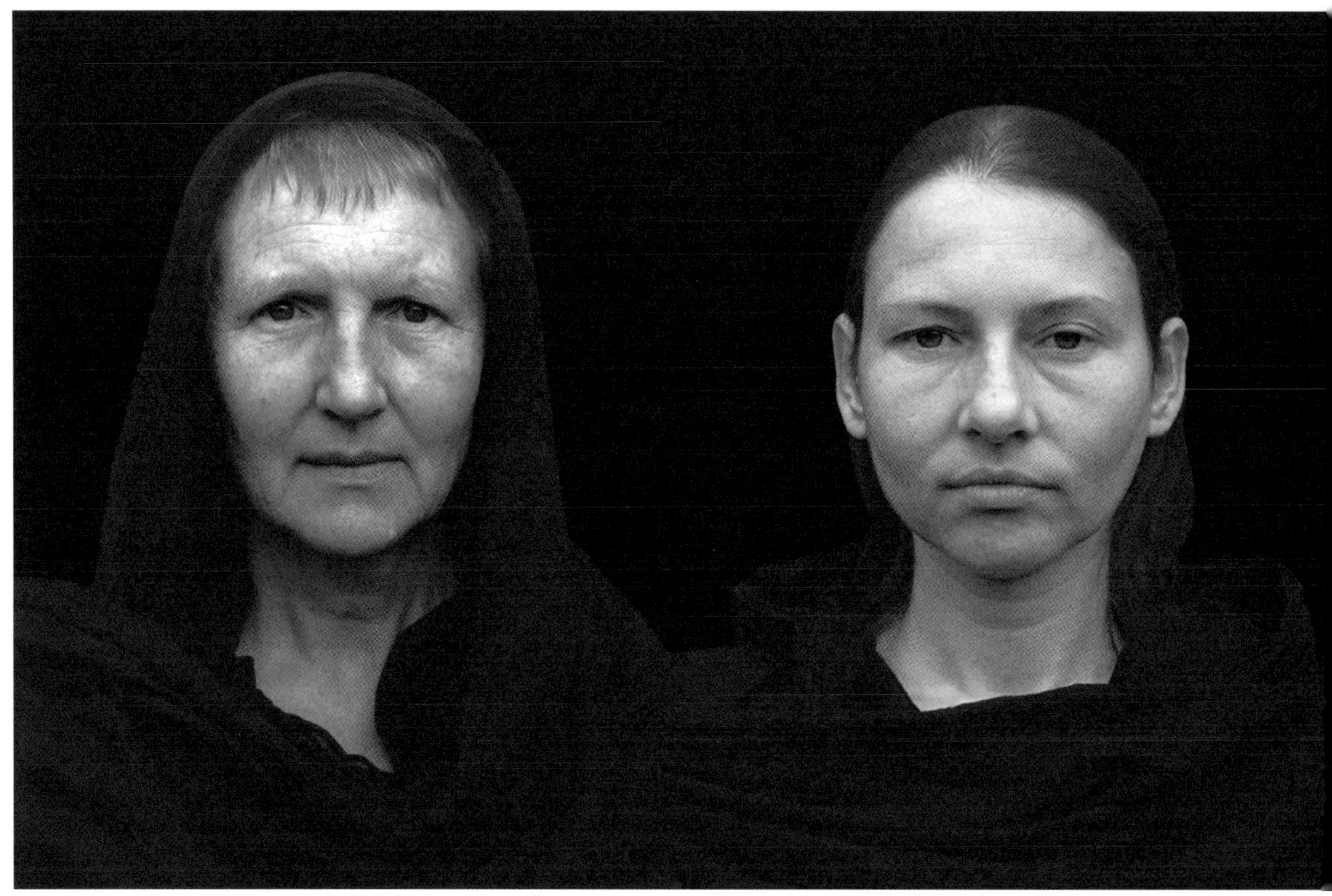

Veil | 1997 | Slide projection installation

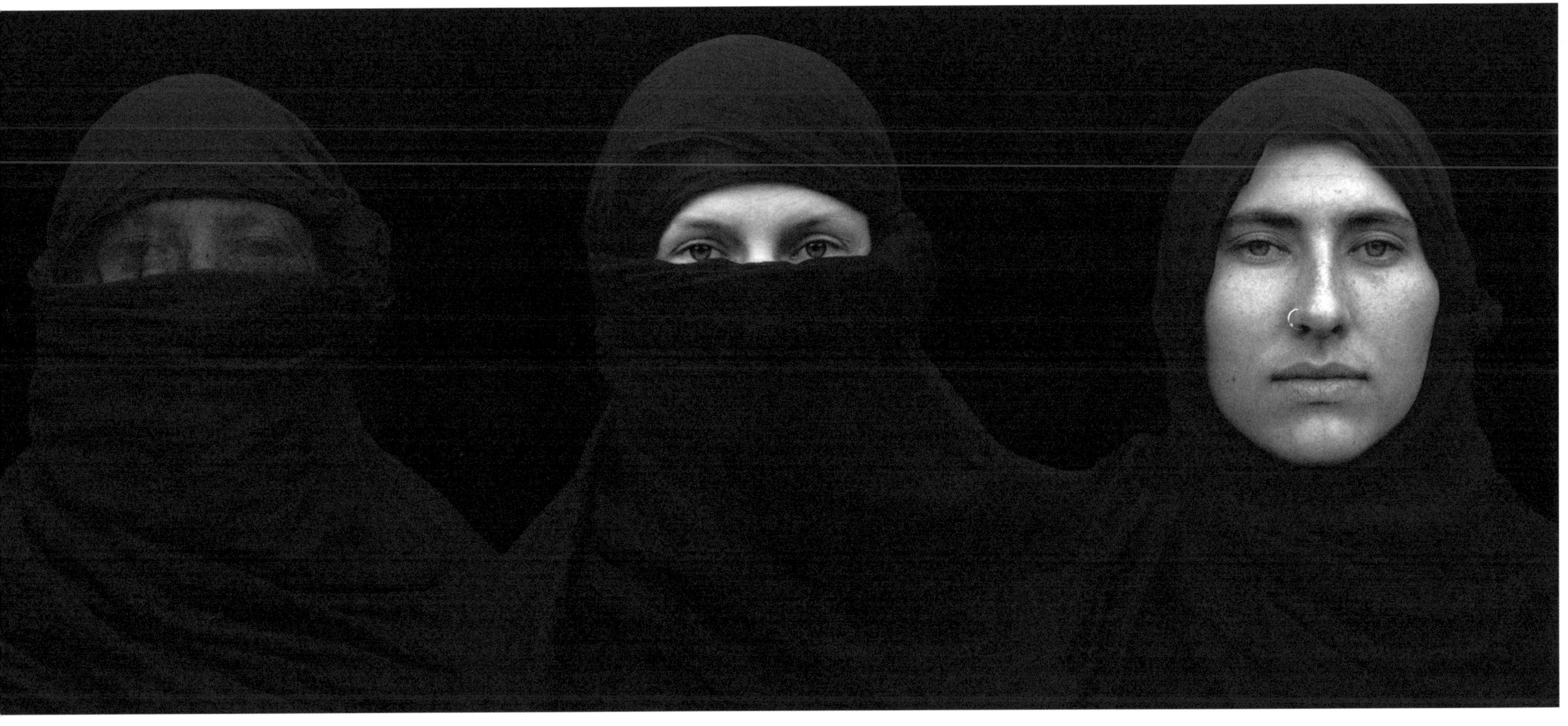

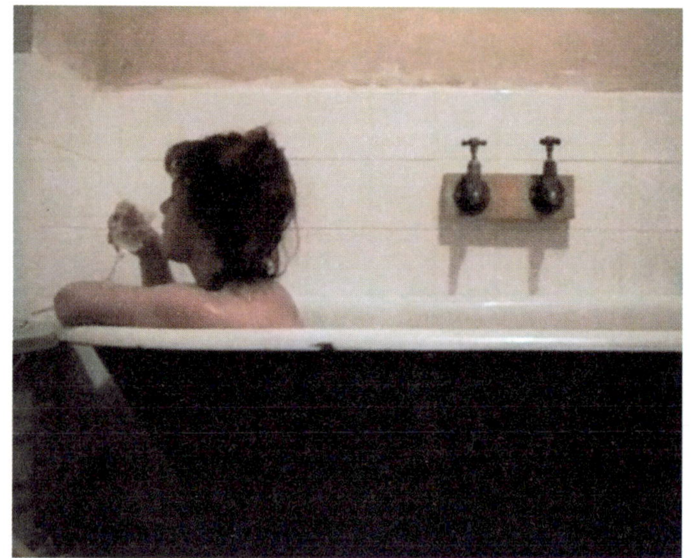
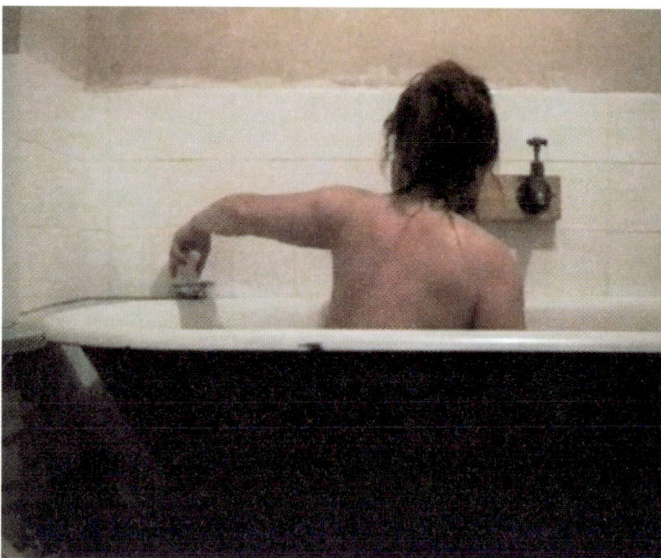
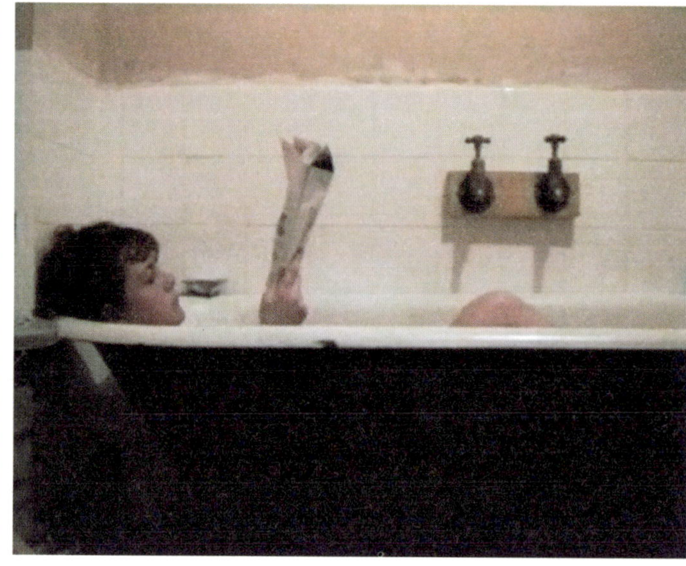

The King's Chamber | 1998 | 3 minutes

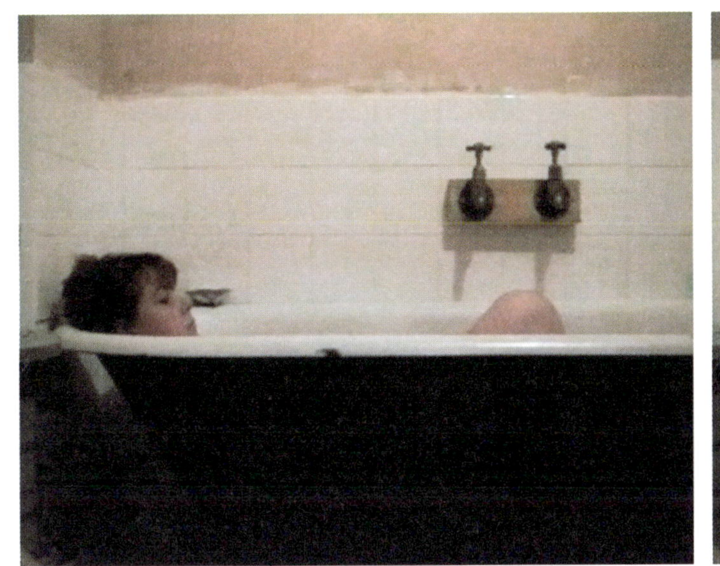
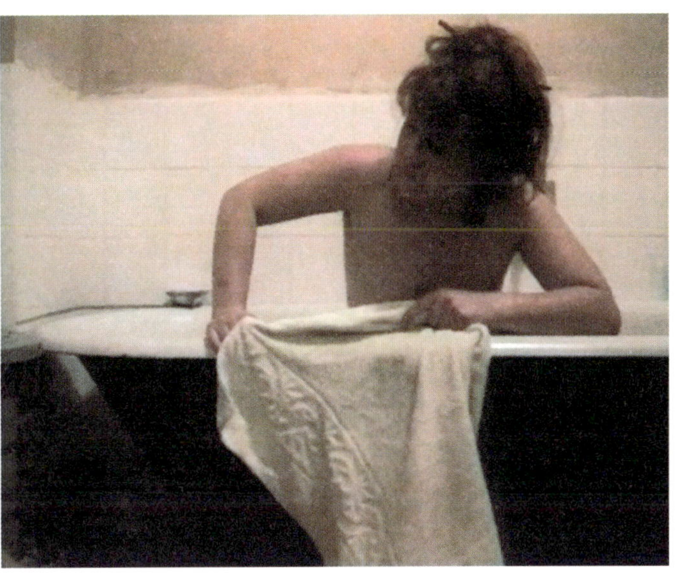
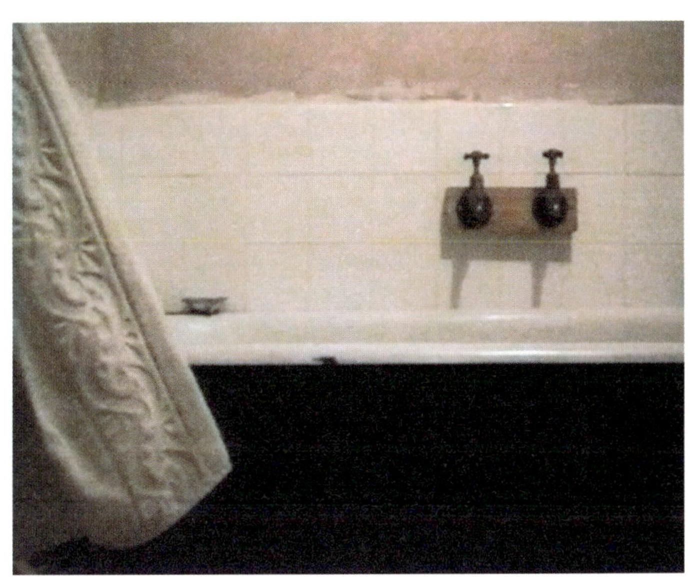

1001 Nights | 1998 | 6 minutes | Commissioned by Margaret Harvey Gallery

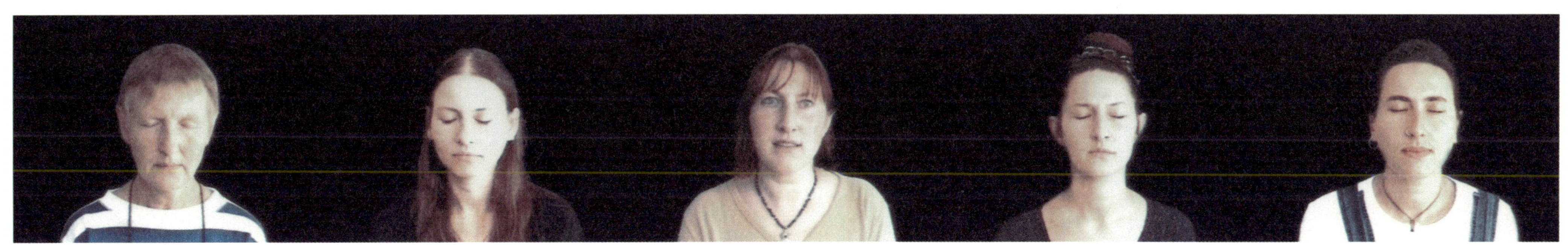

A Loving Man | 1996/9 | 15 minutes | 5-screen video installation | Commissioned by Imperial War Museum

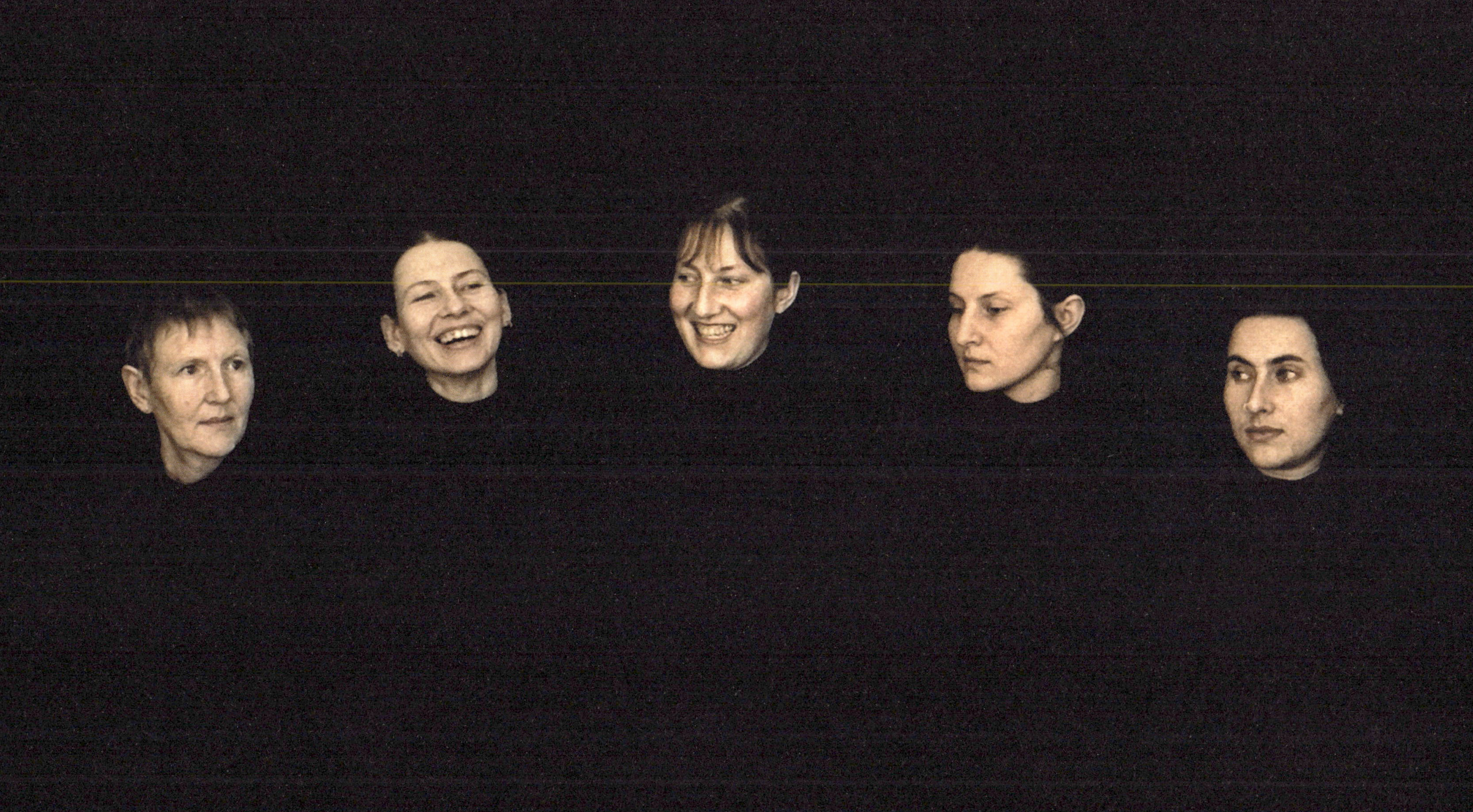

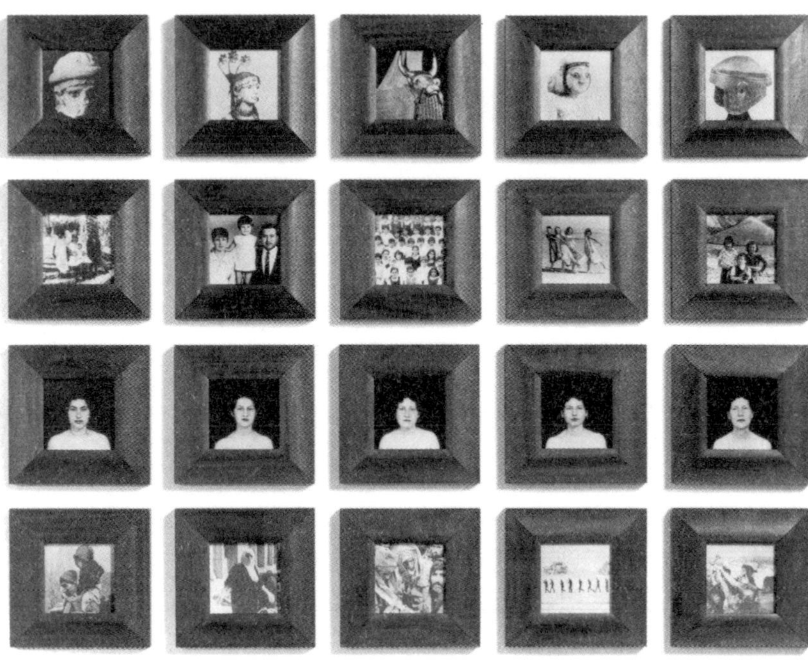

Untitled (Gulf War Work) | 1991 | 20 silver gelatin prints | 100 x 80 cms

It is a Friday morning in early December and we are on a train to Norwich. Once out of London, where it was clear and bright, the landscape is soon wreathed in a thick ground fog. Grey-green fields, the tops of trees and hedgerows appear out of the whiteness, at the limits of visibility. This view out of the train window is very beautiful. The obliteration of detail creates a delicious lightness of being, and a faint excitement.

Norwich is not fogbound but it has that emptiness on a weekday morning which seems so strange after London's incessant busy-ness. The Norwich Gallery is also empty, but the journey has created a surprisingly easy transition, somehow minimising the sense of displacement that occurs when one steps out of the everyday into the zone of an artwork.

A vast expanse of stony, anonymous desert. A lilac ribbon of heat haze ripples along the distant horizon. There is a faint roaring noise, resembling the sound of passing traffic; perhaps we are at the edge of a road, perhaps approaching a border, or we could be in the middle of nowhere. After ninety seconds the scene fades.

The heat haze has burnt off and nothing moves in the desert. The only feature in this landscape is a small gully, edged with a few bushes. In the middle distance, a man, not young, walks into shot from the right. He is too far away for his face to be visible. He is wearing an old-fashioned double-breasted suit and the desert wind blows his trousers against his thin legs as he walks. He strides vigorously across the terrain, turns his back to the wind, lights a cigarette, waits, continues walking, a sliver of shadow at his feet. Why is he here and what is he waiting for? He walks out of shot in the direction from which he came.

The man reappears from the left, walks away towards the gully until he is only a spot in the distance. He returns. It is hot but his jacket remains buttoned up, and his trouser legs flap in the wind. He walks away out of shot.

A sequence is establishing itself. The man again walks into shot from the left, walking more slowly, circling aimlessly, smoking, staring at the ground as he walks. His shadow is beginning to lengthen. He disappears out of shot and we gaze at the desert as the sound of traffic continues intermittently.

The horizon is a dusky mauve. The man wanders backwards and forwards, more tentatively, occasionally kicking at stones. His wait seems increasingly futile. The wind never ceases. His shadow is now taller than he is.

The man walks into shot from the left, tethered by the long black line of his shadow. When he turns his back to the sun and wind, his shadow precedes him tirelessly.

The light is fading. The man is standing in the middle distance. He paces more and more slowly, despairingly perhaps. The wind blows from the west and the man lights another cigarette with his back to the wind and the sun. He stands still, smoking.

The desert is a darker gold, the sky dusky. The man enters left, slowly meandering, pausing, smoking; the arm with the cigarette held down at his side. His evening shadow seems funereal, a black line stretching beyond the frame, a path to nowhere. As the sound of an approaching lorry grows louder and louder, his figure suddenly dissolves as if he too were a mirage. The desert is empty again, except for the continuous whine of traffic along the invisible road.

Muse is a hypnotic piece, yet quite merciless in its disallowal of engagement with the existential figure of the man in the desert. He seems trapped in a dilemma about which we know nothing. The camera's rigid objectivity records eight ellipses of real time from dawn to dusk, but this sequencing could be a metaphor for the passing not just of a day but of a lifetime, each entrance and exit made on the stage of memory.

Whereas *Muse* is a study in longing, frustration and the inability to act, *Echo*, a four-screen video work in an adjacent space, exudes playfulness and intimacy. In contrast to the single large screen of the former, *Echo* consists of four small adjacent images projected at the size of a TV monitor. The basic material of this work was recorded some time ago, then put aside. Sometimes the artist allows work to lie fallow like this, until the time is right to use it.

Four women – the artist and her three sisters – discuss the relationships of someone to whom they are all closely connected. It isn't necessary to know the full biographical background, and the overlapping, interrupted dialogue deliberately inhibits too easy an identification of each voice with the speaker. At first the viewer strives to overcome this fragmentation, but the beauty of the piece lies in the abstract musical interplay of the voices as they express relief, surprise, criticism, disillusion or acceptance. Al-Ani has always resisted a purely biographical reading of her work. Discussing her first major video piece, *A Loving Man*, she said:

> *In the script for* A Loving Man *it was very important to be as vague as possible about 'biographical specifics'. There are actually very few clues in the work to indicate who is being spoken about, where these people are from, what their relationship to each other is. For me that's very important. Otherwise it would be too easy for the work to be read in a wholly biographical context, the whole thing about where the artist is born, what their nationality is — all those particulars are in danger of becoming the subject of the work. This is exactly what I am resisting by being non-specific, it's possible for there to be a way in for an audience that has no intimate experience of some of the things the work is talking about.*[1]

Each woman is filmed in black and white seated in front of a curtain, as in a studio or photo booth. Their body language engages the eye just as the pattern of voices engages the ear in an aural dance. Each woman adopts a different posture; hands twiddle with earrings, a cigarette, a toy on a stick. The woman playing with the toy displays unconsciously childish behaviour, which is lovingly tolerated, just as the artist accepts 'mistakes', like the woman in a black dress who walks behind one of the speakers while she is being filmed. The movements and postures of the body, whether performed as in pieces like *Reel* and *Cradle* or unconscious as in *Echo*, are responsible for the work's visual texture while the voices carry the narrative.

Framing and distance are critical elements in portraiture and particularly so in Al-Ani's work. Frame and distance determine the viewer's position in relation to the image and condition our involvement in the camera's gaze. She has spoken of how in much of her work 'the intention is to make viewers aware of their position... viewers are made to feel as if they are intruding on something private.' In *Echo*, as in *A Loving Man* and *She Said*, we are drawn into an intimate conversation, but held at a certain distance by the withholding of information and the position of the camera.

Muse and *Echo* seem unrelated at first, although the fixed camera position is common to both. Emotionally one is cold and distant, the other warm and relaxed. But the warmth in *Echo* comes from the women's relationship to each other and the fact that they have become more at ease with performance in the eight years that have passed since *A Loving Man* was made. The discourse itself is far from comfortable, nor does it achieve any kind of resolution. Al-Ani has said with reference to *A Loving Man* that.

> *It's also about the way in which events in family history are constantly recollected and even through these recollections, are transformed. And how although memory is something constantly invoked, it is still unstable and unfixed from the moment and constantly being re-examined.*[2]

This is a refreshing attitude, since memory is all too often regarded like an old snapshot, something that doesn't change, only fades, leading to a guilty and futile struggle to remember things exactly as they were. Memory is replete with lies and illusions.

Muse is the first major work in which a male figure rather than a female one occupies the stage, and the first to be shot outside the studio, although the desert is as neutral and unyielding as any studio interior. But at the same time, one can project upon it any number of fantasies. The father figure, an invisible presence in *A Loving Man*, seems to have surfaced, but only to find himself in purgatory.

In 1991, at the time of the first Gulf War, Al-Ani made *Untitled (Gulf War Work)*, an early photographic piece consisting of twenty small square images arranged in four rows of five, framed in wide black picture frames, not the narrow black frames that were once standard for photographs. (Frames, like clothes, speak volumes, and are to the image as clothes are to the body). *Untitled* uses four photographic methodologies: the museological record of archaeological artefacts; family snapshots taken in Iraq, including one of the artist with her parents; consciously styled and posed portraits of the artist, her sisters and mother and press photos of the war culled from newspapers. In its brevity and simplicity it is a poignant expression of history, memory and loss.

While it may seem like a minor work in comparison to the subsequent video installations, *Untitled* is a progenitor of the concerns in *Muse* and *Echo*. The portrait photographs, each expressionless face isolated against a black ground, intimate the direction Al-Ani's work would take, and what it would leave behind. But perhaps the figures in the landscape are after all the most telling, both those in the family photos and those from the desert war in 1991. Rather like coming across an old trail in the forest, the artist crosses it, marks the spot and moves on.

The train draws out of Norwich station after rain. Suddenly a brilliant rainbow appears in the sky. This ravishing mirage doesn't fade away in mid-air as rainbows usually do, but expends itself deep in the Friday afternoon silence of the city's industrial outskirts as the train carries us away.

1 Jananne Al-Ani interviewed by Gill Addison in *Filmwaves* magazine, 2002
2 Op.cit.

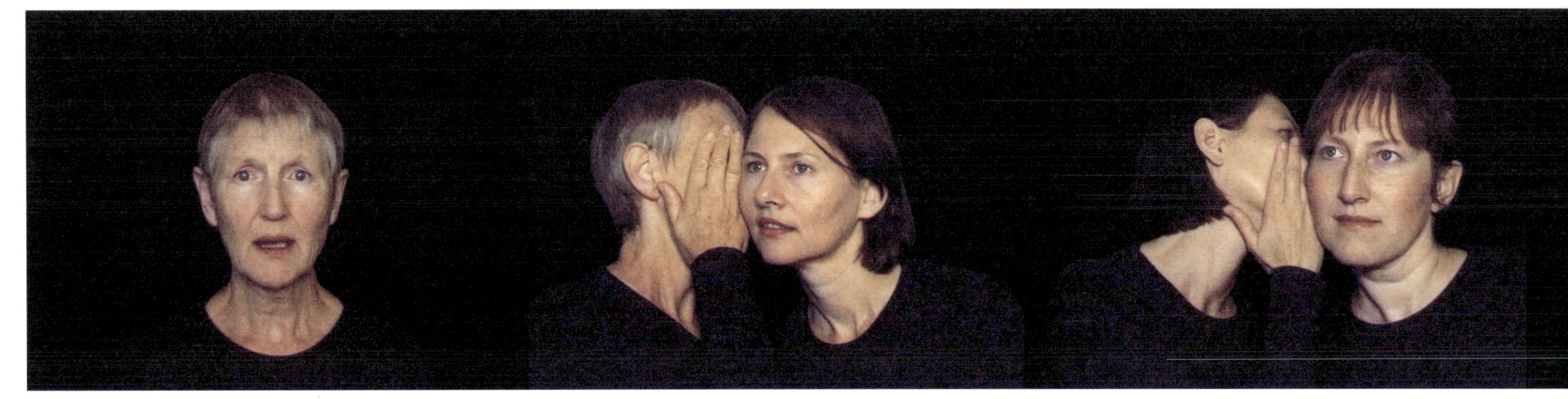

She Said | 2000 | 22 minutes | 5-screen video installation | Commissioned by The New Art Gallery Walsall

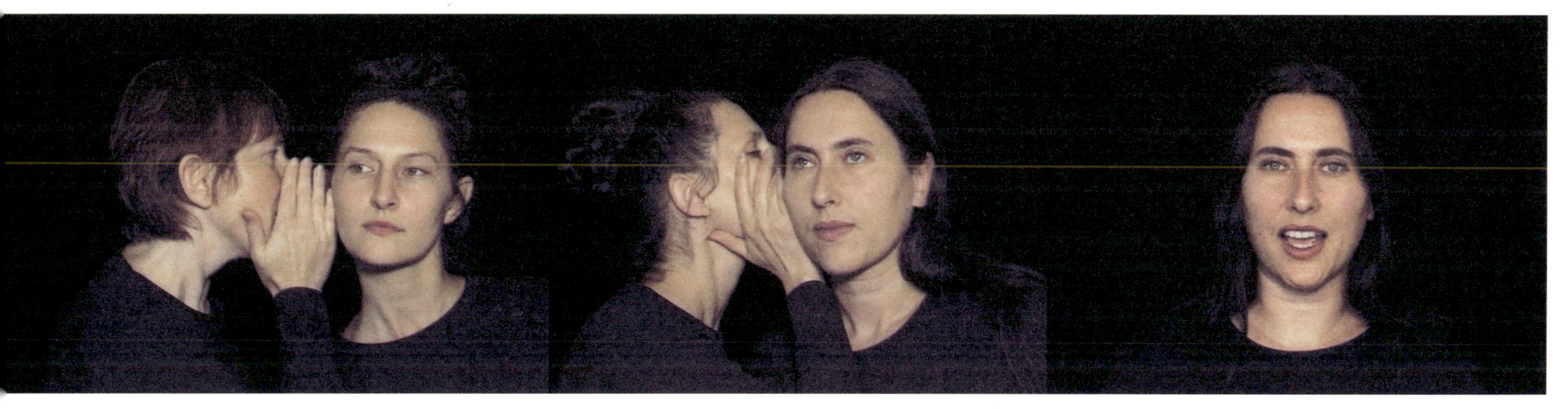

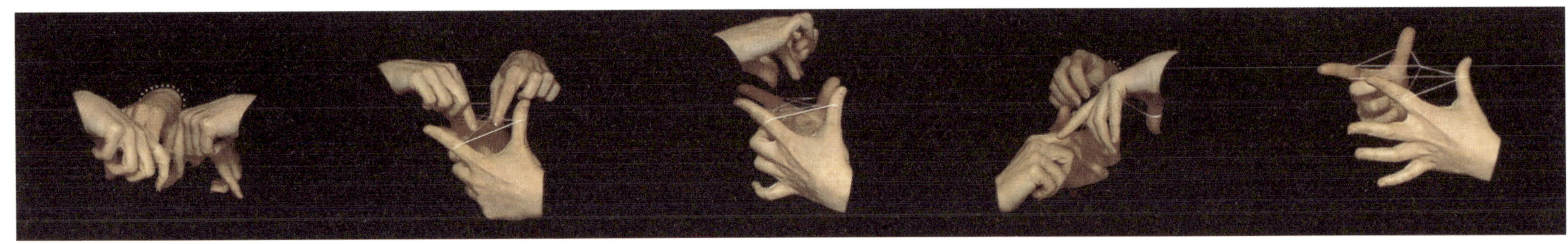

Cradle | 2001 | 2 minutes

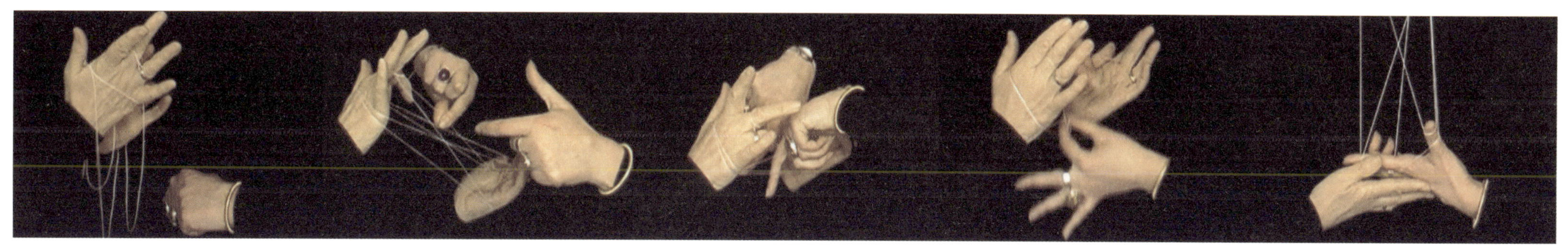

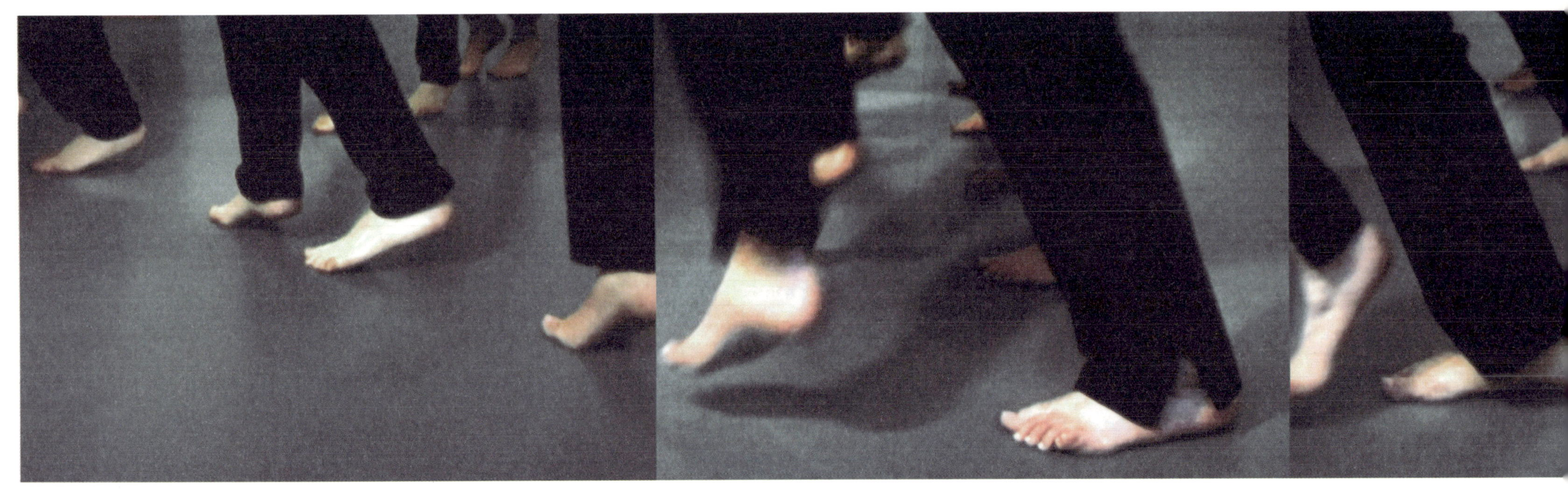

Reel | 2001 | 2 minutes

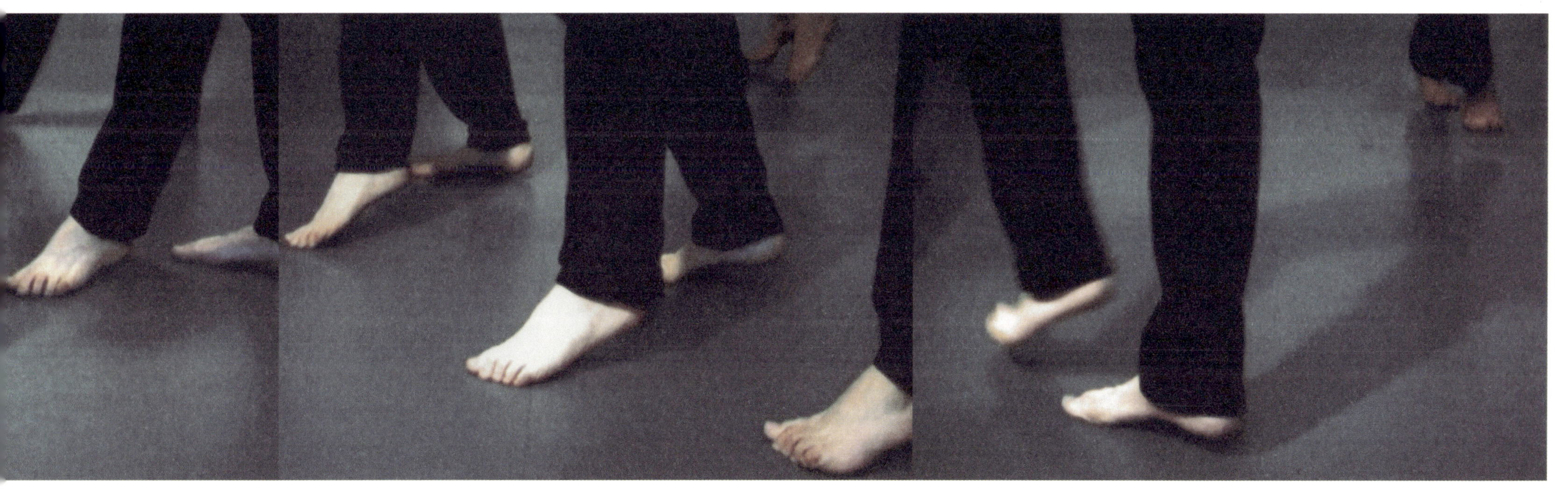

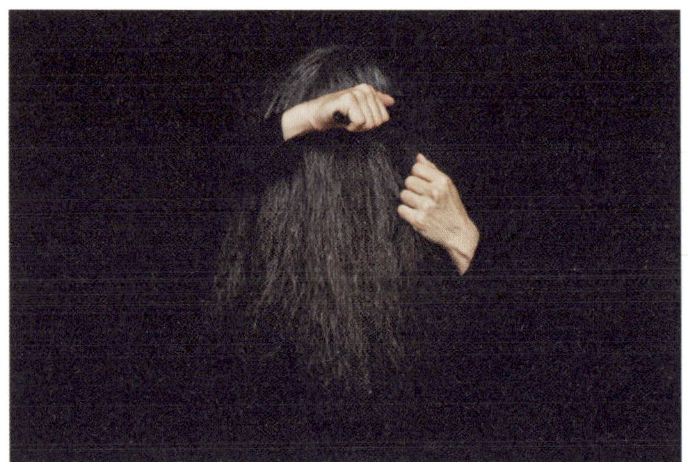
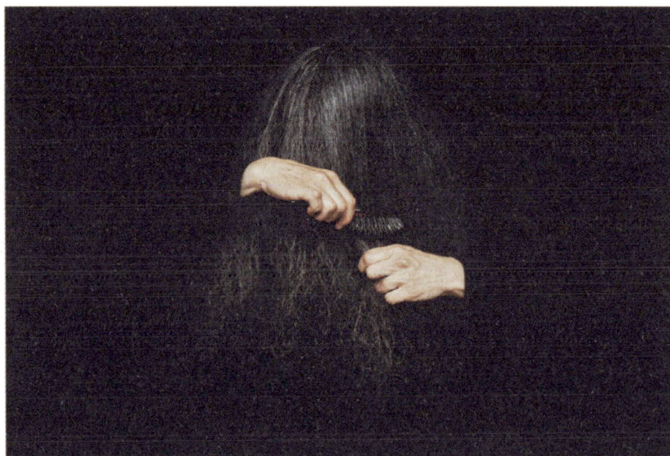
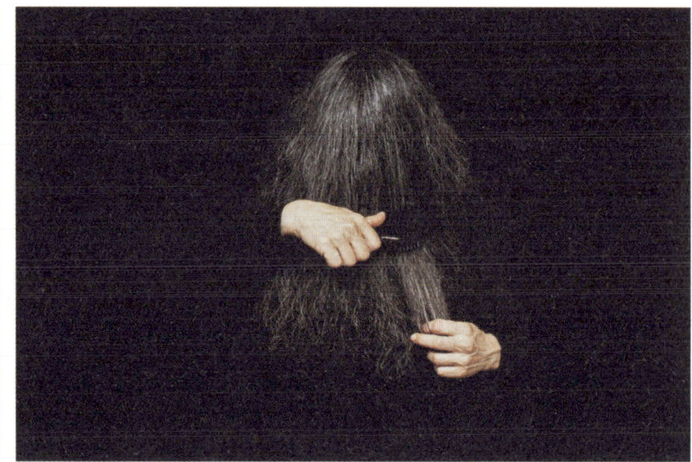

Untitled | 2002 | 3 minutes | Commissioned by Terra Incognita

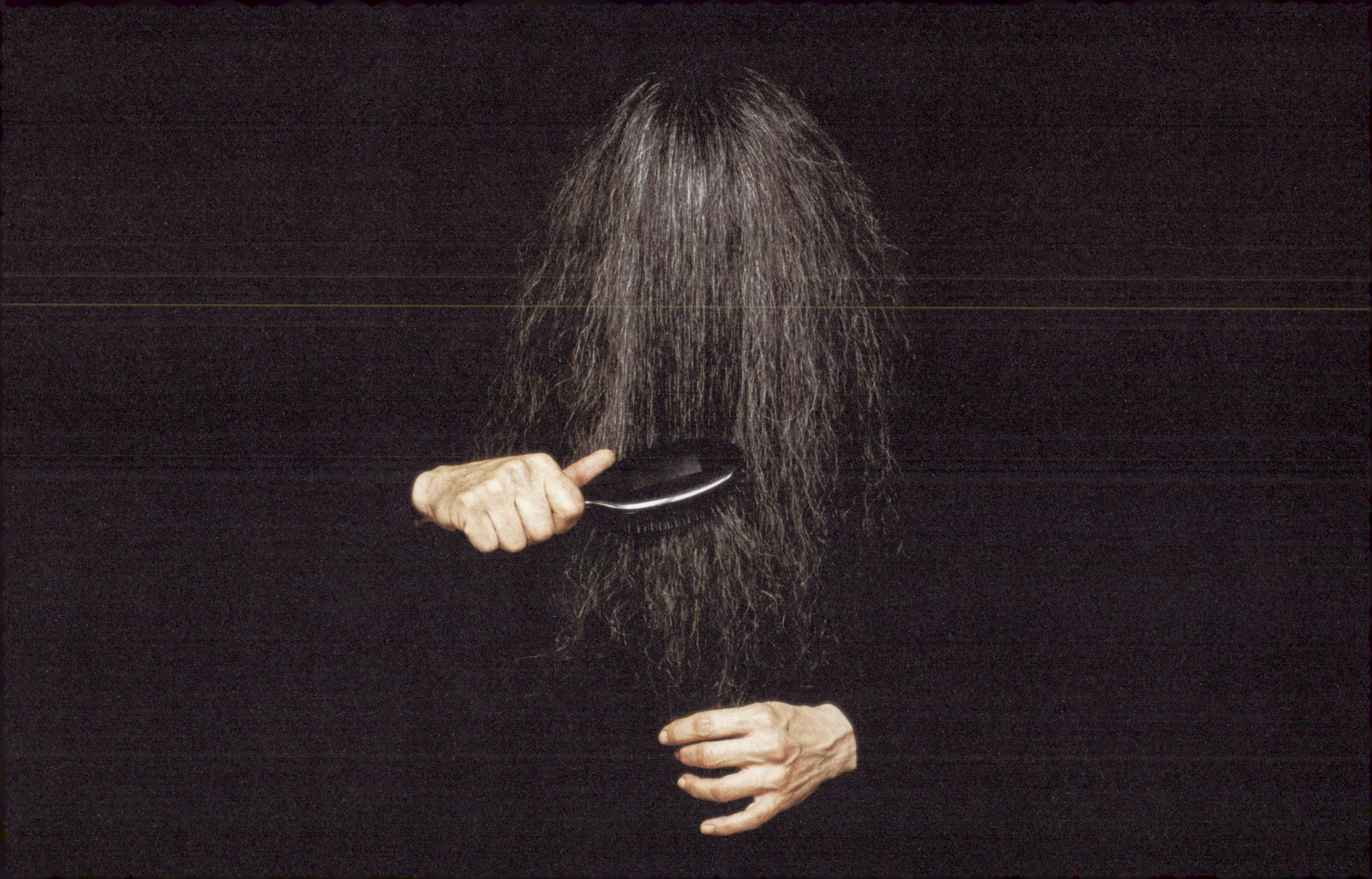

Richard Hylton interviews Jananne Al-Ani

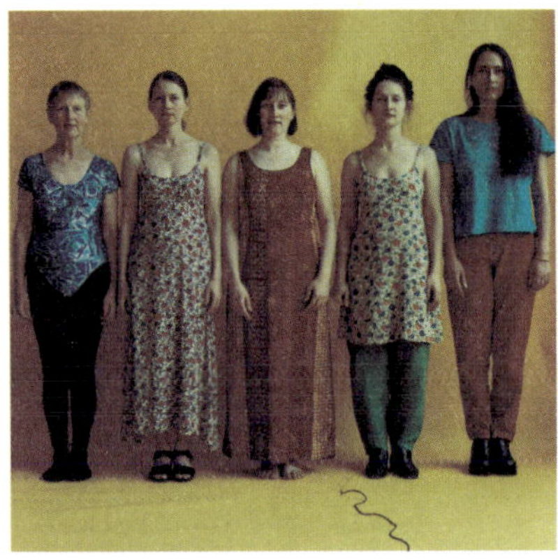
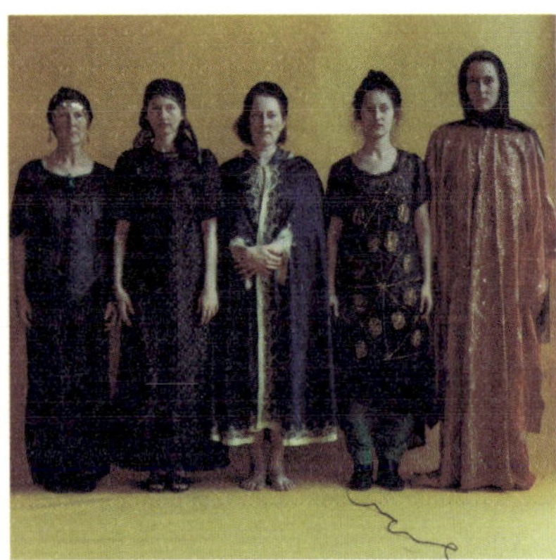

Untitled | 1998 | C-types | 120 x 120 cms

Richard Hylton I wanted to start by asking you what it was that attracted you to photography, and why it continues to play an important role in your work?

Jananne Al-Ani Well, initially, I was more interested in painting and I was using photography as a way of sketching and either drawing or painting from photographs. As an undergraduate I was encouraged to think about using photography and video instead of painting, because it seemed, to some of my tutors at least, that they were more appropriate media for work which was politicised in some way... so I resisted using photography, because I was so fixated on proving them wrong. It took me the best part of my degree course to reconcile the fact that I was actually more interested in working with photography and the moving image...

RH Could you talk a bit about the *Untitled* group portraits of your mother, sisters and yourself?

JAA I'd been interested early on in looking at Orientalist painting but it was only later that I discovered a whole body of photographic work which was produced during the same period — what you might call a kind of Orientalist photography. I was particularly interested in images which focused on women as the subjects, but also the relationship between the photographs and the paintings. The paintings are very clearly fantasy, a fiction, and could be very extreme in their constructedness, whereas the photographs, somehow, because they had this relationship to reality and the document, did something very different from the paintings; as if the photographs became evidence that the Orientalist fantasy really did exist in the flesh.

RH How do you see the use of photography itself as a medium which can equally be a kind of veiling device because of the idea that it represents 'truth'?

JAA The idea that photography is a mirror of reality says a lot about the way in which Orientalist photographs were consumed in contrast with the paintings. One of the things I discovered when examining images of Middle Eastern women in late 19th and early 20th century European photography, was a book by Malek Alloula called *The Colonial Harem*. He was looking at photographs produced in Algeria from the late 19th century to the 1930s, of Algerian women: photographs ranging from the ethnographic to the pornographic, in which the women are gradually undressed and revealed. He drew a direct analogy between the veiled woman's gaze and the gaze of the photographer, and he said that the photographer was infuriated by the veiled woman because he recognised her gaze is his gaze, the photographic gaze.

RH Do you see the subject of your work being about photography itself?

JAA In part, yes. In the photographic work I've done on the veil, I'm certainly not talking about the veil in a sociological or anthropological way — it's simply a visual device; it appears and disappears. What's important for me in the work is the returned gaze of the women; the fact that they're all staring out of the picture in a very confrontational way, so that the relationship between the female subjects and the viewer is undermined in some way. My intention is for the viewer to become self-conscious. In the photographic work and the video installations I try to manipulate the viewer into making them aware of the physical space created by the work. So with the black and white photographs of five women in various states of veiling and unveiling, the two images are shown facing each other, so that when the viewer enters the gallery they are in the space between the two photographs and they are interrupting the women looking back at themselves in a way. It's very important for me where the viewer is positioned within the physical space of the work.

RH In your photographic work you've sometimes used binaries signifying representations of Middle Eastern and Western culture. You've also presented pairs of photographs. What informs your decisions for employing such devices?

JAA Well, firstly, I would argue that the works you are referring to are not about an East/West binary but about the construction of that binary through Orientalist art and literature. The works play with images and motifs taken from Western painting and photography, which say nothing about the reality of life for women living in the Middle East at the time and everything about fantasy and fiction. As for the use of pairs, I guess it's about the idea of not having a singular anything, so you have five women in an image, not the one or two you might normally expect to see in a 19th century studio portrait. I'm interested in the idea of the group or the community. So when we stand in front of a painting like the *Rokeby Venus* or the *Naked Maya*, there's room to fantasise about a potential relationship between viewer and subject. When you look at a photograph of a group of women, especially ones staring out of the picture in a rather confrontational way, I think it does something completely different to the viewer.

RH Your family, and to a degree your father, have played a crucial role in your work. Where do you see the relationship between personal and more social narrative concerns coinciding in the work?

JAA I don't think any of it is personal narrative. I think the work gets read like that because I'm often using my family as the performers, and sometimes I'm using family histories or stories, as starting points for the work, but actually that's not what I'm interested in. I mean, I don't see any of these works as being autobiographical or biographical. I'm much more interested in the idea of narratives evolving and shifting and changing and exploring our relationships to histories and the way those histories are in constant flux...

So, for example in *A Loving Man*, a man is being talked about in the third person by a group of women, and although it's myself, my mother and three sisters on screen, most of our comments are quite generalised, and despite the apparent intimacy of what's being said, I'd like to think the work generates a certain empathy in the audience because most people have at some time experienced difficulties in relationships with the men in their lives.

RH In previous interviews you've spoken about the process of making work changing over the years. How has it now developed?

JAA Very early on I was photographing my mother and three sisters regularly, but I didn't consider the photographs to be part of my work as an artist it was more of a personal document and it was two or three years before I started photographing myself with them. The first work I ever incorporated these portraits into was *Untitled (Gulf War Work)*. From then on this linear motif of the five women appeared regularly in the work and we have developed a process that's closer to the way a group of actors or a theatrical troupe might work.

RH Why did you decide to use your family, then? You talk about the personal not being so important, so in the photographs or in the videos, why do you use your family as opposed to actors?

JAA Well, I suppose it came out of that very first piece, which was about trying to introduce a more complex historic narrative into the events of the first Gulf War, and also to bring the body back into the landscape. In the press coverage of the first Gulf War the body was totally absent, we saw aerial shots of the desert... photographs of an empty landscape. So the idea was to include the formal portraits with snapshots from the family album and photographs of ancient Mesopotamian archaeological artefacts, and last of all a series of documentary images appropriated from newspapers. So I guess this early appearance of the family was a way of personalising or humanising the war but in later video works like *A Loving Man* or *1001 Nights* they become more like actors whose job it is to deliver much more complex and often ambiguous narratives.

RH But when you work with them, how much detail do you go into, and how much of the work is made prior to you actually asking them to be involved?

JAA Well, when I was making photographs, we had much more of a traditional artist/model relationship where I ordered them around. I would have quite a clear idea of what I wanted them to do before I got them into the studio, and then I would simply set it up and photograph. But since I started working with video, the process has become much more collaborative, and it's partly because I've become more interested in exploring this idea of constructing narratives and histories, by introducing the voice. The work has become much more like theatrical improvisation, so there isn't a predetermined script, there's just a loose idea, and I'll introduce them to that idea.

For example, in *1001 Nights*, each person was asked to recite a recurring dream that took place in Iraq. That was the only stipulation and each of them was left alone with the camera rolling. I then collected all the material and edited it together. Until I'd viewed the material after the recordings were made I had no idea what any of them were likely to have said yet it looks like there's a consistency that runs through the stories, which is there by chance totally; it's not something prescribed, I didn't have any control over it. Sometimes I'll set a task and the results might not be very interesting so I won't make use of that material; other times it works, like in *1001 Nights*, and it's possible to make a piece out of it.

RH In terms of moving from photography into working with video and sound, you can control things in both areas, but how would you say that working with video has changed your way of working? I mean, it strikes me that in pieces like *A Loving Man* and *1001 Nights*, for example (I'll get on to some other work later), it's seemingly quite controlled, but actually when you watch it, you leave in all the laughter...

JAA Yeah, they're amateurs, and that's actually really important. The fluffed lines and the mistakes and the awkwardness of the performances are actually very important to me. I think the work explores the relationship between the still and the moving image, which is very clear on a formal level: but it also occupies a strange space between the unpredictable nature of live performance and the perfection of filmic performance. It's really vital for me that my cast appear to be the amateurs that they are, and to still be thinking about the ideas as they're going through their performance.

RH I suppose that's a kind of literal reading on my part, in terms of the idea of humour, where your sisters are giggling away. But one of the things that occurred to me... is this idea that, because of the way they're filmed, and because they're all good-looking women...

JAA You're very kind, too kind...

RH No, no, because you've often talked about desire and the Orientalist image, etc. How conscious are you of that? Because obviously they're very well-composed images and the ones where you're whispering [Laughter]... I can't think of a way to put it...

JAA But the thing I like about that particular piece (*She Said*), and the reason I think it works, is the way in which our affection for each other is so palpable in our interactions on screen. I think it's quite different from works like *The King's Chamber*, which tackles voyeurism and desire in a very explicit way...

RH On this issue of representation and visibility... to what degree do you think the work could perpetuate ideas of desire or intrigue?

JAA What's seductive about the work isn't the women *per se*, I think it's the obvious intimacy between the characters that's compelling.

RH But what does that do to the viewer, then?

JAA Well, for me it's not about exciting desire so much as making the viewer feel excluded — which is what I've tried to achieve in *A Loving Man* and *She Said*. They are both shown in small, dark, circular spaces. As a viewer you're interrupting something that seems very private and intimate. People often stand on the periphery, at the entrance to those installations, they don't go right into the centre of the work. When you are in the centre, it's as if you're intruding or eavesdropping; you shouldn't really be there, because the women are so engrossed...

RH Yes, but if you're in the centre, surrounded by these women, you could say that it's also quite a good space to be in — I mean, speaking as a man.

JAA I don't know. I think it tends to undermine the audience more than make it feel like pleasurable voyeurism, which is something I am interested in. You know, the idea that traditionally in works of art where women are the subject, the viewer is in the privileged position of voyeur, being able to look without being seen; and that the structure of these works does undermine... Oh, I can see what you're saying: you're saying, well, it could be the opposite; it could be like the ultimate... like being in the harem or in the Turkish bath.

RH [Laughs] You said that, not me. No, I don't mean it like...

JAA No, you said that.

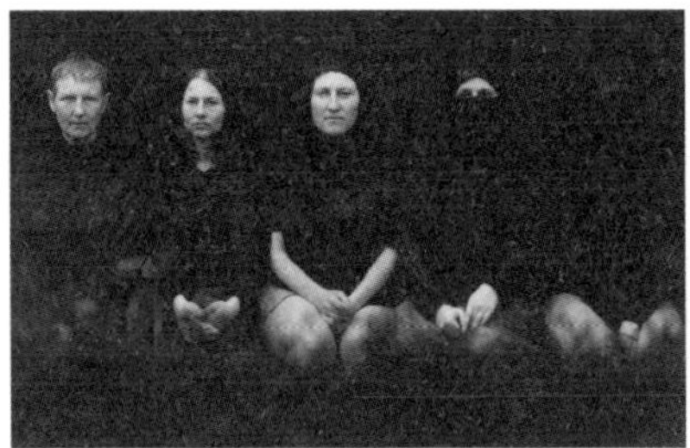

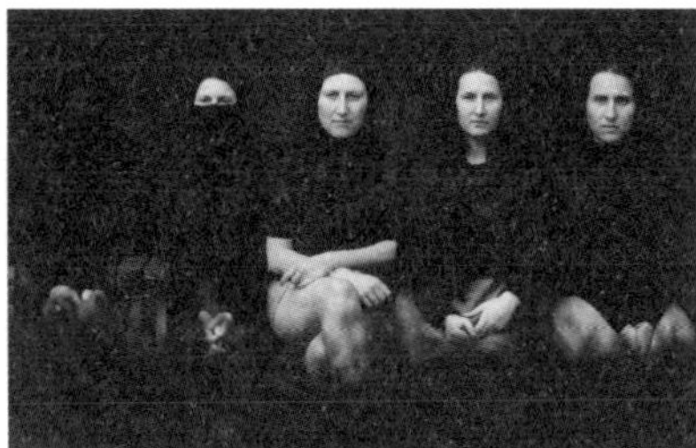

Untitled | 1996 | Silver gelatin prints | 120 x 180 cms

RH No, I didn't say it's like being in a...

JAA Or potentially.

RH Maybe I'm reading too much into this, but it makes me think about the idea of fantasy and desire and using the female body to try to challenge that?

JAA I think this raises interesting questions about how much control artists have over the consumption of their work. Talking about whether the work invokes desire or not brings to mind the long-running debate amongst Feminist practitioners in the 60s and 70s about representing the female body. Although many artists refused it, arguing that it was beyond redemption because of the way it has been abused, others, like Hannah Wilke and Carolee Schneemann embraced it and made challenging work using their own bodies, some of which is still controversial today... I guess it's pointless to make assumptions that your work is going to be read in the way that you intend, and, if there's a critical element to the work, that it's going to be understood.

RH What would you say are the motivations for making quite different types of work, like the portraiture in *1001 Nights*, and the more anonymous use of the body in pieces like *Reel* and *Cradle*?

JAA They're different formally, I know, but then they're similar in other ways. For example *She Said* and *A Loving Man* are based on word games. *Cradle* and *Reel* are also based on recognisable pre-existing structures which relate to games and play and although they're silent I think they both still say something about the idea of communication. I suppose many of the works are a reflection on the way a community or group of performers functions. Those which feature 'talking heads' seem to be preoccupied with portraiture but I think both *Cradle* and *Reel* and even the video piece with the woman endlessly brushing her hair over her face are in some way oblique portraits.

But I'm still interested in the amateurishness of the performance and the possibility of failure. So, for example, in *Cradle*, there are two sequences: one where the players are very efficient and quickly conclude; while in the second sequence one of the players clearly doesn't know how to play and, without that knowledge, there is no progress. It's a doomed performance. And it's the same with *Reel*, despite the apparent coherence of the dance; if you watch the feet carefully, there are some performers who are more proficient than others, and some who are clearly following.

RH How important is the order? There's an order to your work within the frame, but do you feel that you like to control things?

JAA Yes, I do — overly, I think. I'm trying very hard with this new work to move away from that, which is kind of ironic, because, in my experience, filming on 16mm is a much more laborious and slow process than working with video. You know, I thought I was being much looser with this new work, but actually when I had to reconcile the process itself, I realised that it's even more controlled and contrived than the way I would normally work. So I guess that's just the nature of making work; at some point you have to make a commitment to what you're doing and just go through the practical process of getting the material shot.

RH Do you want it to come across as being quite controlled?

JAA No, I just can't do it any other way. [Laughter]

RH Well, you're being honest about it...

JAA That's why I love painting and drawing, because there's a kind of fluidity that you don't have with lens-based work. You know, the idea of sketching; although I do sketch with the camera but it's not the same...

RH I was just wondering how you feel that works in terms of working with professionals.

JAA Well, it's actually really liberating because you can rely totally on their expertise, but it does mean that when you get to a certain point you have to be clear about what you're doing... I think the camerawoman I worked with on *The Visit* was shocked at how blasé I seemed to be about the whole process; my ideas about what I wanted to shoot were quite vague and I didn't have a storyboard or anything like that. You know, it's a huge commitment financially. And yet when we were actually on the ground filming, I was very clear about what I wanted her to do and it worked out well.

RH Do you feel quite privileged to be working in that way?

JAA Yeah, it's fantastic, absolutely fantastic. I have employed camera and sound people in the past for some of the more complicated pieces like *She Said* when it became impossible to perform, direct, film and record sound, which is how I'd always worked before. To be honest, it's been a real eye-opener working on this commission. Having a generous enough budget to allow me to employ the expertise I need to produce new work on film has really highlighted the level of poverty most artists work at in terms of access to resources and skills.

RH I was interested in talking partly about the idea of commodity. I think it was Martin Coomer in *Time Out* who said of your work — it's the sort of work that wins awards...

JAA I wouldn't mind if it was true but the work he was talking about hasn't won any awards! [Laughter]... But he wasn't talking about the market at all was he? When artists receive 'awards', it's quite different from being commercially successful and it's much more likely to be seen as a political move, isn't it? He was referring to *Veil*, the large slide projection installation, which was made in 1997; though I think it's significant, looking at the review, that it was being shown after September 11th. Maybe he thought the work would appeal to closet Orientalists or perhaps he was suggesting that awards are only given out by the art establishment to artists who are seen as outsiders in some way, when it is politically expedient to do so and not because the work has any intrinsic merit... I've heard enough moaning about the 'privileges' given to particular artists to know that positive discrimination is a popular myth in the British art world. To be honest I've no idea what he meant, you'll have to ask him...

RH I mean, it's a kind of banal comment in many ways, considering the art that does get promoted on a daily basis in the media...

JAA What I think is interesting is the way in which artists from 'elsewhere' are more often than not defined by their biographies and not by the work they produce. At the other end of the scale we get to know everything about establishment artists' likes and dislikes: where they shop, what they feed their cats, what their favourite colour is... I'm not sure which is worse!

RH In recent years you've been travelling more extensively to the Middle East. How has your work been received there?

JAA When I was invited to participate in the *Home Works* Forum in Beirut in 2002, I hadn't exhibited anywhere in the Middle East so rather than just doing a talk about my work I also focused on the research I'd done as co-curator of the *Veil* exhibition. I thought it would be a challenge to see if any of the issues raised would be of any interest in a Middle Eastern context.

RH And what was the response?

JAA The audience was very generous but, as I suspected, had many reservations — making work about Orientalism and the veil is just not that interesting for Middle Eastern artists. You know, if I was working there, I would probably agree. In Lebanon there's a really lively community of artists whose work is really interesting and varied and a number of them are becoming increasingly prominent on the international art scene.

RH But how does it compare to here, then?

JAA Well, as is usually the case, artists there know all about what's happening in the world and in the West; the problem is, not many people here know what's happening there. So they're actually in a much healthier position, because they have a very wide perspective on what's going on in terms of contemporary practice; they know what's happening regionally and on an international scale, so they're much better informed. What they don't have is a well-developed infrastructure or decent access to resources and expertise.

RH How has that affected your thinking about your work? Because obviously you exhibit in Europe and North America...

JAA Yeah, I do, and if anything, the work is just as differently read if I show it in England and Sweden as it would be in England and Lebanon. On the other hand I do think some works could suffer being misread depending on the context in which they are shown.

RH In your new work you travelled to the Middle East to film.

JAA Yes, I was looking for a generic desert landscape to film in which I guess brings us back to the work I was talking about earlier, the photographic piece made after the Gulf War of 1991. At the time it was a revelation to find that the Orientalist stereotype of the desert was still deeply embedded in western thinking about the Middle East. It was this notion of the desert as a blank canvas, one on which all kinds of fantasies could be projected, which appealed to me. I want to re-occupy that space in some way.

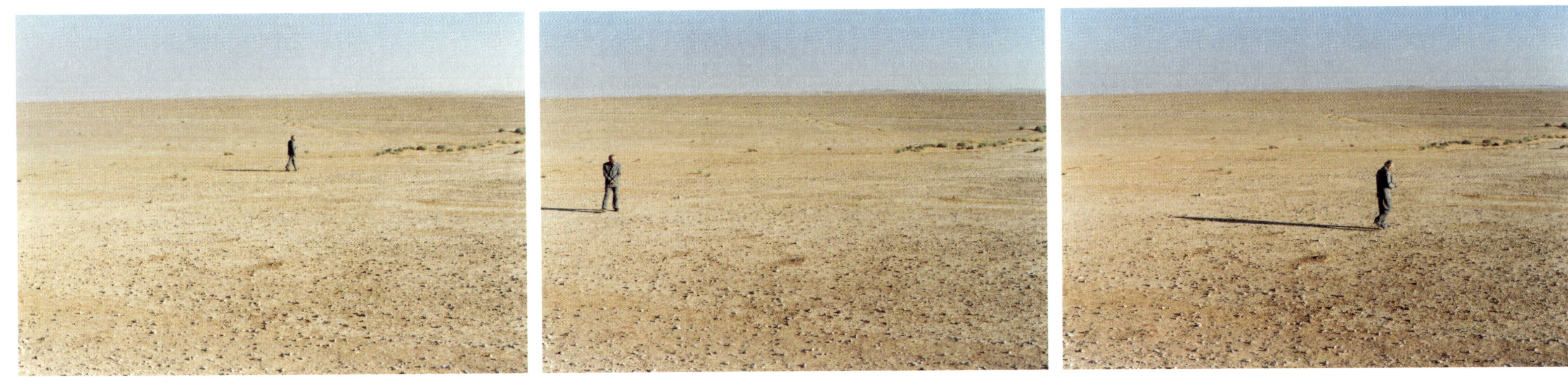

Muse | 2004 | 15 minutes | Commissioned by Film and Video Umbrella and Norwich Gallery | Photographs Effie Paleologou

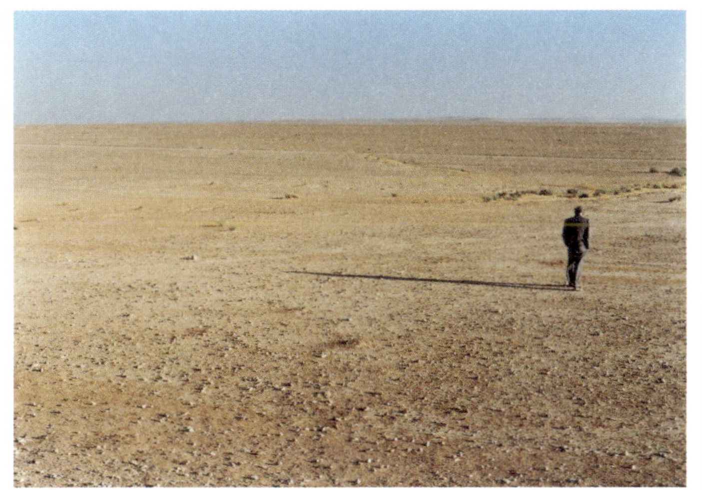
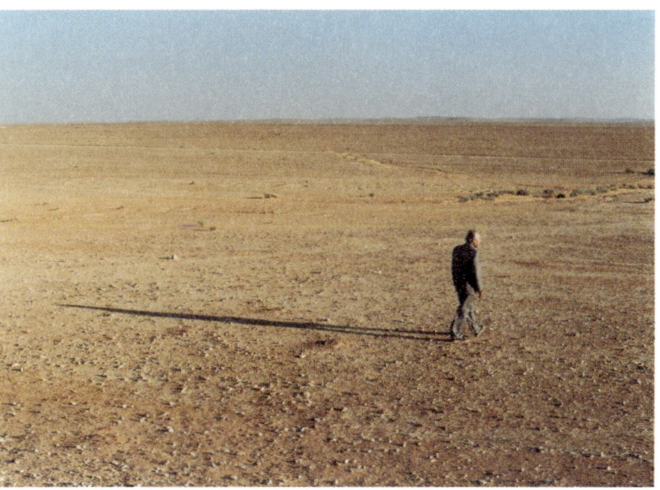
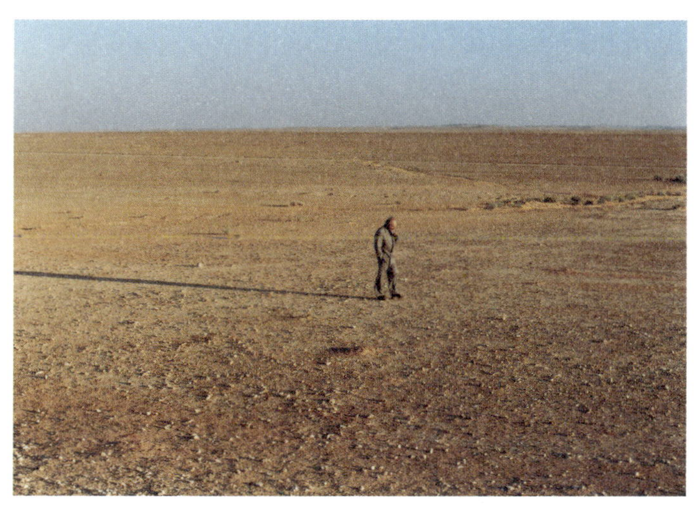

Muse | 2004 | 15 minutes | Commissioned by Film and Video Umbrella and Norwich Gallery | Photograph Effie Paleologou

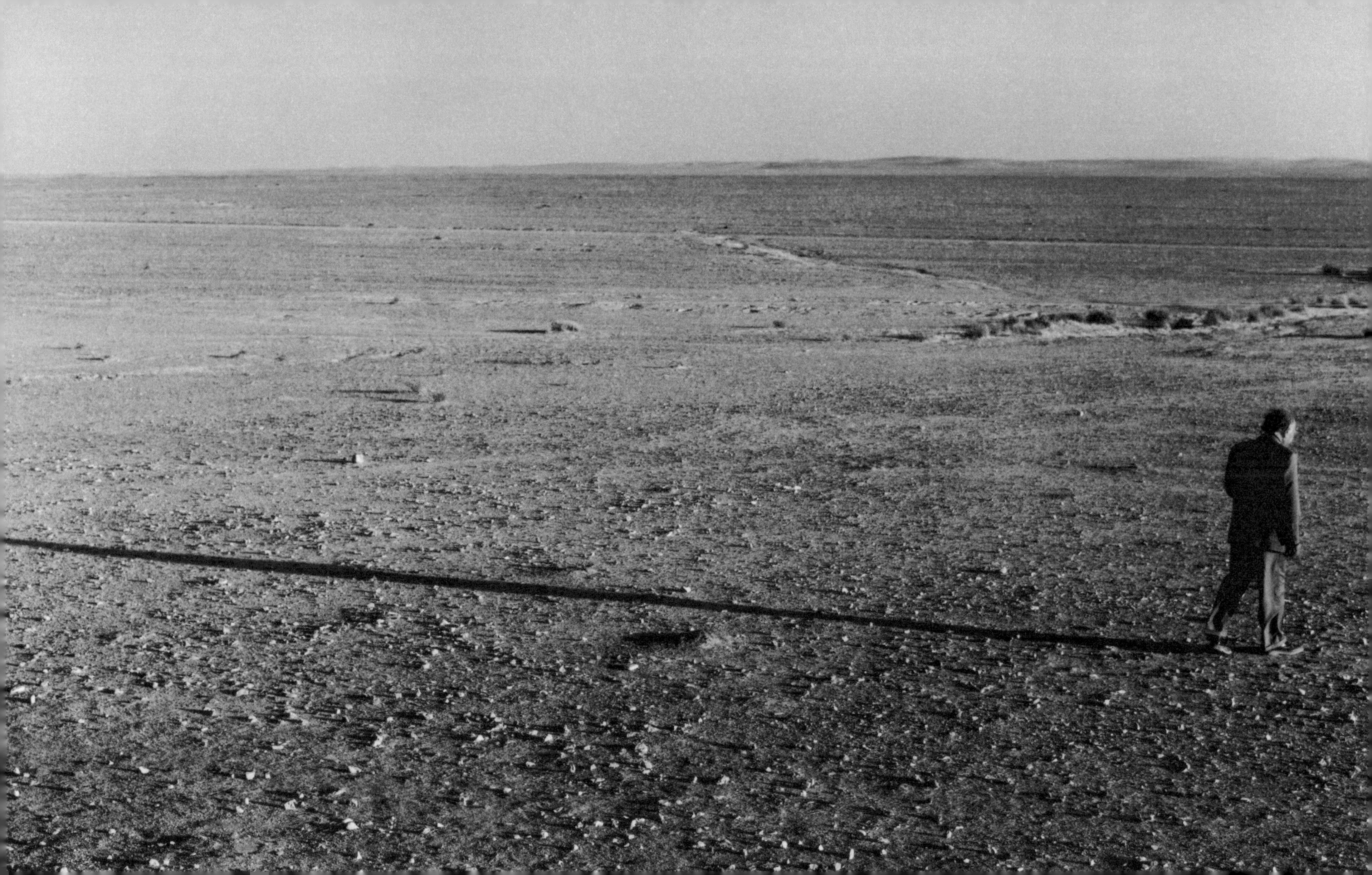

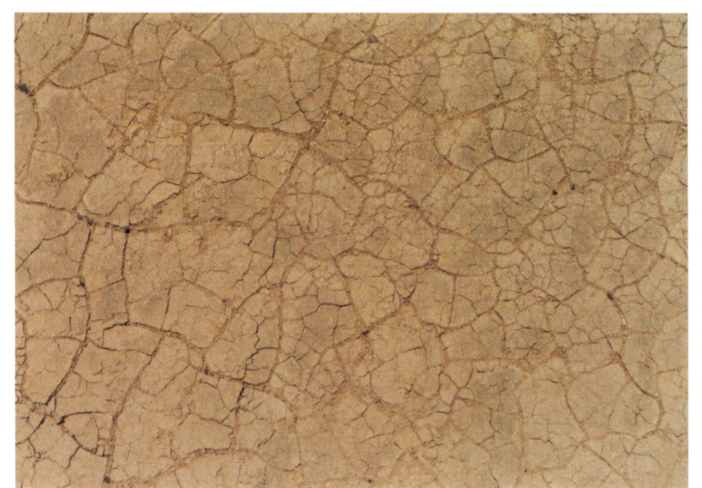

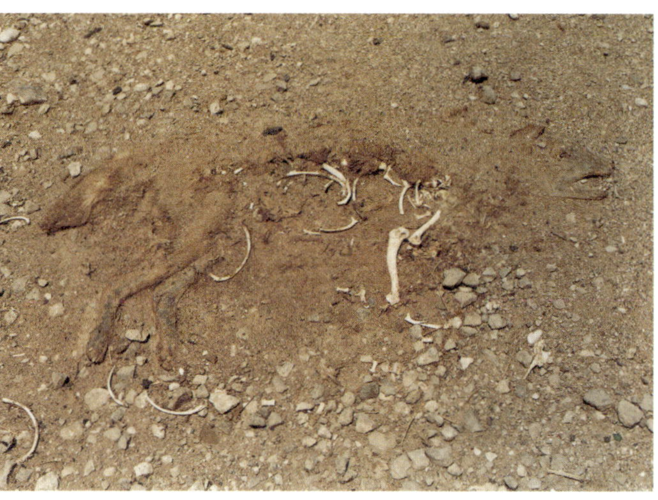

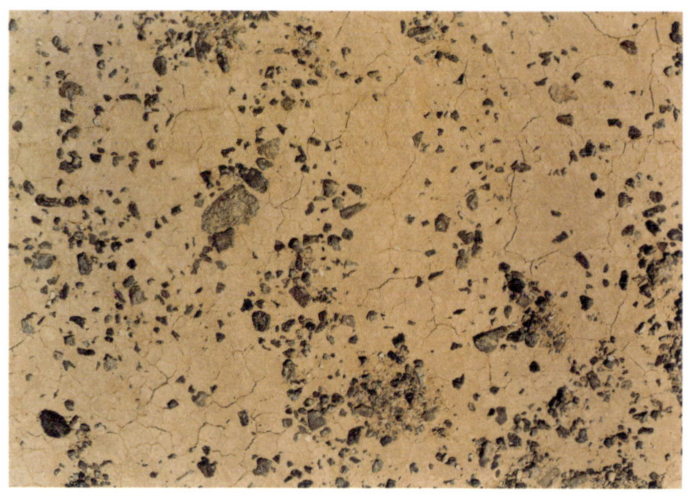

Muse (location stills) | 2004 | Commissioned by Film and Video Umbrella and Norwich Gallery | Photographs Effie Paleologou

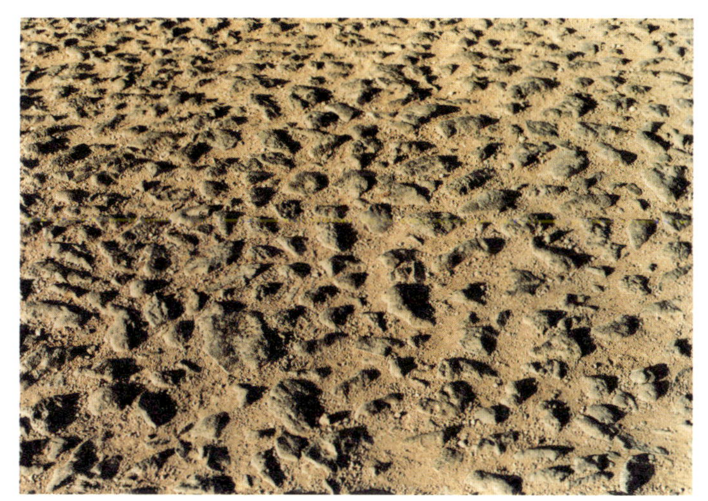
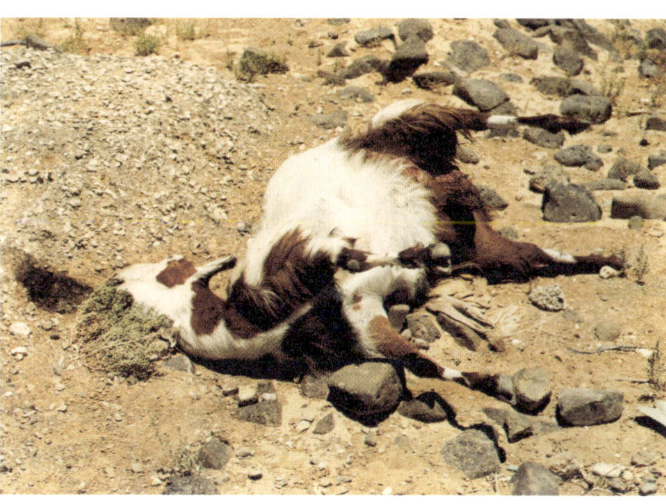
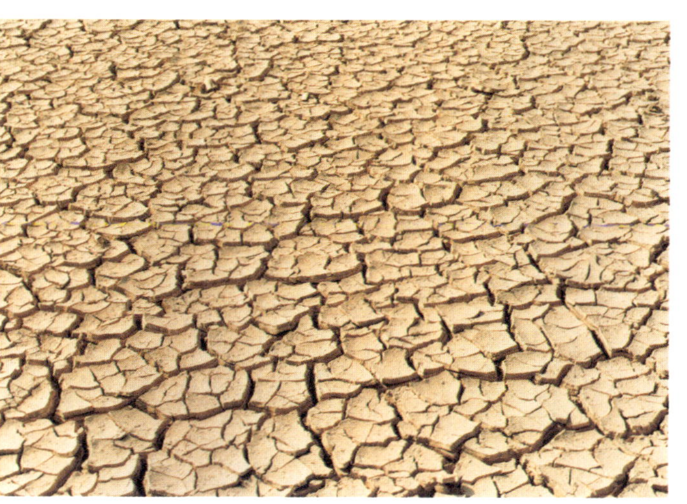

Echo | 1994/2004 | 10 minutes | Commissioned by Film and Video Umbrella and Norwich Gallery

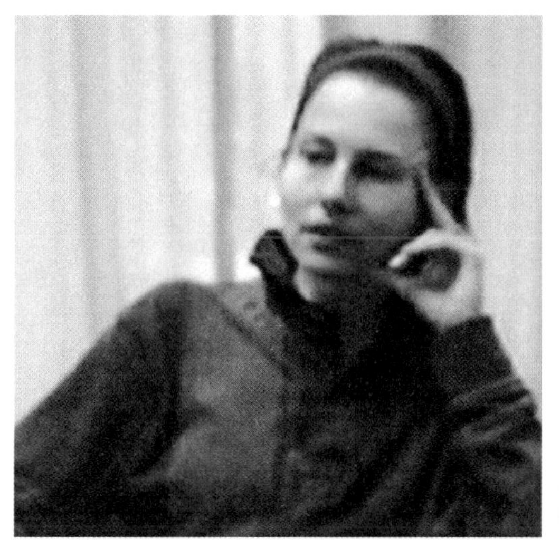
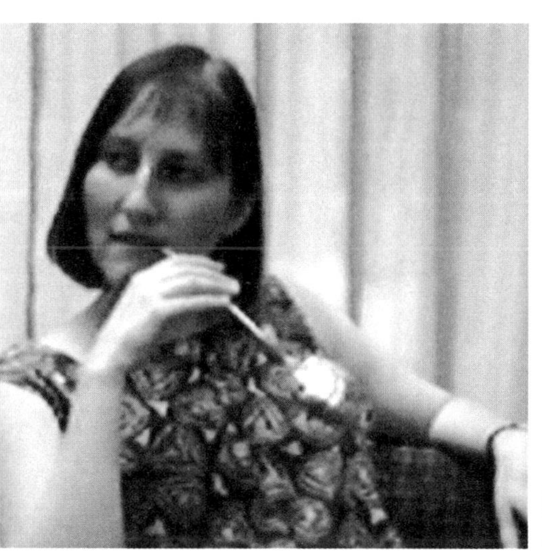
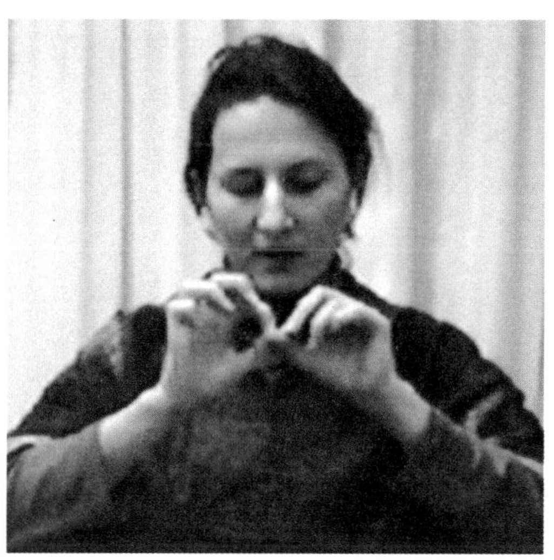
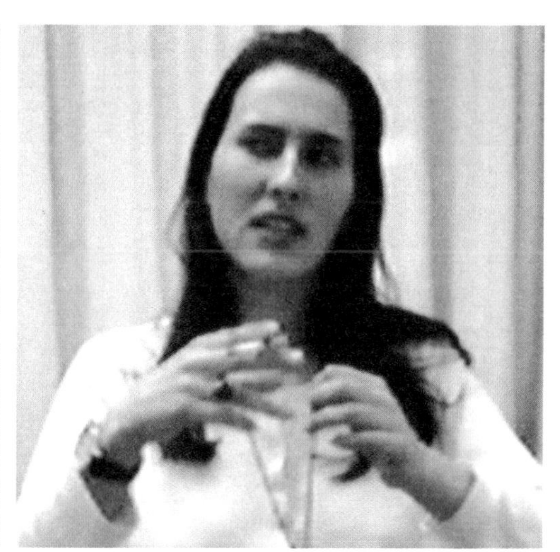

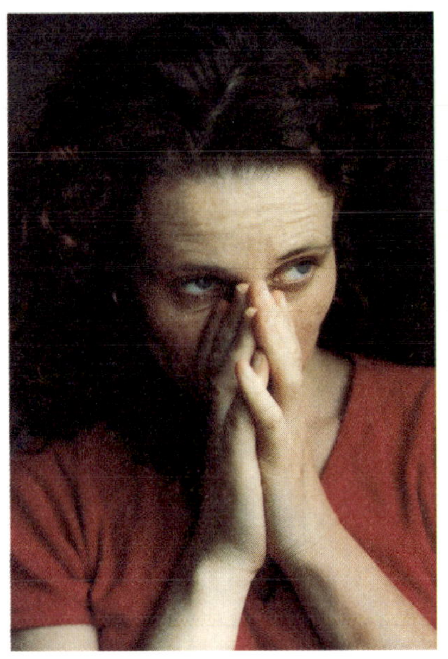
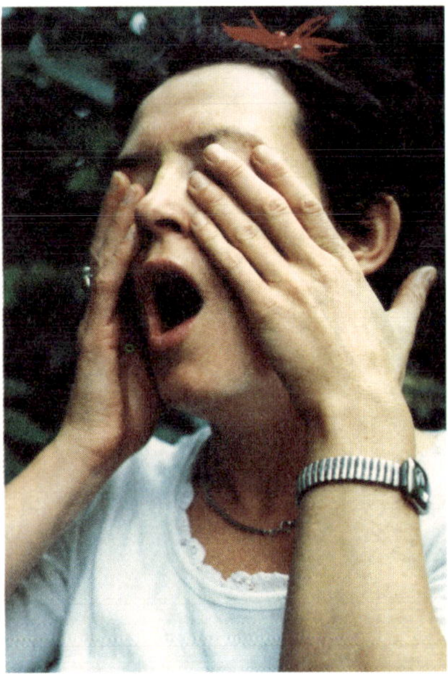

Portraits | 1999 | Duratrans and lightboxes | 20 x 25 cms | Commissioned by Imperial War Museum

The conflict on which a tragedy is based must ideally be one where there is no possible resolution.

Johann Wolfgang Von Goethe, on *Interpreting Aristotle's Poetics*, 1798

Tragedy illustrates the universal rather than the particulars of history — illuminating through catharsis what is possible and what can likely happen in the future.

Micah Garen, on *the Looting of the Iraq Museum*, 2004

Aristotle's definition of tragedy, proposed in 4th century BC, relied on a denouement involving a central figure, who should display neither purity nor immorality. Rather, the tragic protagonist should commit an act of *hamartia* (an involuntary mistake or sin), so their inevitable downfall would be played out through a series of wrong turns or deviations. 'Tragedy,' Aristotle argued, 'is an imitation of an action that is serious, complete, and of a certain magnitude... in the form of action, not of narrative; with incidents arousing pity and fear, wherewith to accomplish its catharsis of such emotions... Every tragedy, therefore, must have six parts, which determine its quality — namely, Plot, Characters, Diction, Thought, Spectacle and Melody.'[1]

Tragedy, then, is not narrative, but drama, built through the contrivance of complex characters. Aristotle named Euripides as the most tragic of poets and it seems that it is to Euripides that contemporary theatre has instinctively turned during the past year in the aftermath of the Iraq war. Euripides exhibited an iconoclastic, rationalising attitude toward the ancient myths that were the subject matter for Greek drama, relating them to the political climate of Ancient Greece. Three revivals of his tragic plays have occurred on the English stage within a year of the onset of the War on Terror, leading one critic to observe,

It is the Greek understanding of the human consequences of war and

of the gulf between public rhetoric and private feeling that makes these plays seem shockingly relevant to our own divided world.[2]

Euripides' insistence on accentuating the previously muted voices of women and slaves, in such plays as *Hecuba* and *The Trojan Women*, appeals to contemporary playwrights such as Frank McGuinness, though their direct parallels with such atrocities as Fallujah and Beslan may have been unintentional. The impact of such works lies in the replacement of onstage violence with suspicious fear and gnawing grief, wherein the chorus, Euripides' fickle witnesses, creates haunting, humanist comments on the inhumanity of conflict.

Though the work of Jananne Al-Ani is neither melodramatic nor brutal, the inevitability of Greek tragedy resides in its rhythmic lament, in its darkly-clad chorus of women, in its absent, but ill-begotten 'hero'. As the audience, we are cast between pity and fear, between empathy and anxiety. Since the mid 1990s, Al-Ani's photographic and video portraits have been dominated by the central figures of her mother, herself and her three sisters, and a pervading, yet absent paternal figure. It is only in her most recent exhibition, *The Visit*, that a male character is physically represented, in *Muse*. Yet, even here, he appears as if a mirage, pacing across a wilderness, cut off, distanced, mute, separated from the cacophony of voices or chorus of women in the corresponding projection piece, *Echo*.

The desert landscape in which Al-Ani places the suited man is a theatrical space of dislocation. The only distinguishing feature is an incessant rushing sound, which fractures the exoticism of the parched terrain. Its potential to act as a fantastical space is superseded by its proximity to the noise: a possible motorway, or runway, the non-places of potential travel. It is also the abstracted Orientalist desert landscape — the anonymous antonym to urban civilisation, described by Slavoj Zizek as the real stage on which global economic and geopolitical interests are played out.[3] It is the ground space of a media war, the target of a distant satellite, onto which the West projects fantasies of the absent or unknown. The figure is both protagonist and muse. He is the implicated subject of the women's chatter in the corresponding *Echo*, their inspiration and the cause of their anxiety, yet he remains anonymous and mute, condemned to wait from dawn to dusk.

Though the women converse, they appear trapped by vacillation, their words truncated and overlapping. In Greek mythology, it was Echo's punishment from Hera that she should never again speak first. Critic Jean Fisher once proposed, 'Echo's disembodied voice that speaks in others' tongues presupposes an additional function, it is also an ear. Echo is both audio receiver and transmitter.'[4] And so it seems, in Al-Ani's *Echo*, the women can only refer *ad infinitum* to the absent male(s). Though his voice is absent and his body displaced, their voices are effectively merely echoes of his presence, real or imagined. It is worth remembering amongst the nine muses, there was a muse of tragedy.

Whilst there are obvious correspondences in Al-Ani's works to theatrical performance, she persistently subverts linear narrative and the suspension of disbelief. It would be unwise to read her work simply in terms of its associations with the melodrama of Greek tragedy. By contrast, the staging, pace and vernacular of her previous work seems more closely allied to the absurdist tendencies of Beckett or the alienation of Brecht. Brecht once wrote,

The audience should never be allowed to confuse what it sees on the stage with reality. Rather the play must always be thought of as a comment upon life — something to be watched and judged critically.

Al-Ani insists upon this distance from reality, mostly veiling the immediate surroundings of her subjects, omitting the paraphernalia of the studio, masking or partially covering her and their bodies. This partial view not only alludes to the iconography of the veil, but also serves to isolate the female subjects, so that the intensity of their words, their accents and their facial expressions are heightened. Consequently, their 'comments on life' are abstracted from the specifics of time and place.

It is in Al-Ani's manipulation of language that she moves closest to the work of Beckett. Similarities may be drawn in their use of repetitive phrases and *non sequiturs* ('He Tried. But Did He Try Hard Enough?'); their portrayal of people as creatures of habit who fail to communicate: 'This you may delete at some stage' becomes 'Did it go illegal at some stage.' Just as Beckett's existentialist anti-heroes Estragon and Vladimir are condemned to wait for Godot, Al-Ani's female protagonists seem drawn to a similar fate. Their questions, their games, their whispers, their conversations, their recalling of dreams seem futile in their attempt to resolve their histories, to find a single story or resolution.

Significantly, however, Al-Ani is cautious to disrupt the dramatic tendencies of her work. We are given fragments of conversations, or statements removed from their originating context and though her scripts, staging and filming are precise, the result is edited to appear unexpurgated. Laments are disturbed by giggles or mistakes. The competency of delivering lines or actions fluctuates with each member of the group — the result being that our consumption of the works is ruptured. These are the moments at which Al-Ani's art leaks into the theatre of her work.

So whilst the device of the blank stage or void is used to decontexualise the women, Al-Ani incorporates subtle ruptures to subvert the dramatic logic of the drama. What we experience is multi-faceted, bewildering and frustrating, as truths and fictions become indistinct. Al-Ani knowingly combines a series of factors to perform this layering of modes: the enigmatic use of her biography; her incorporation of the veil literally and metaphorically; her use of the video camera as confessional and her manipulation of language to wrong-foot the narrative, to indicate the partiality of memory.

Her five subjects are never shown in direct conversation with one another, even in *Echo* where they appear to address each other, but in fact are filmed individually. They are complicit in games of listening and repeating, sometimes projected to create a cacophony of opinions and conflicting memories, sometimes shown episodically in such works as *She Said* (2002) or *A Loving Man*. The rhythm of these five-screen installation works rests on the fluctuation between past, present and future tenses:

Everything is censored.
Everything fits together now.
She Said

He was my hero. He was loving and he made me laugh...
He feels deserted by us and we feel deserted by him...
Will he ever love me for who I am...
A Loving Man

What occurs between the exchanges is an oscillation between resolution and denial and between subjects – he, me, and she – which inevitably leads to lapses in memory, understanding or tone. The game, like that of mastering the cat's cradle or the steps of a reel in two works of 2001, provides a structure which, effectively, veils the meaning of the words, or perhaps their direct familial associations. Just one spoken line – 'when politics, religion, war and cultures clash, it's the ordinary family that pays the price' – indicates the geopolitical context in evidence in Al-Ani's early work. Her award-winning portrait of 1996 (John Kobal Portrait Award) and her slide installation *Veil* explicitly explore the assumptions surrounding the representation of the veiled woman in Western culture. Though viewed now from the anti-Muslim turmoil of the post-9/11 World Order, these images are still negotiable and perplexing. As Al-Ani's co-curation of the exhibition *Veil* (2003/04) reveals, the myth of the subjugated sexualised 'oriental' woman as object may be challenged by a reading of the veil as a mechanism for seeing without being seen.[5] As the gaze of the viewer is resolutely returned by the subjects in the slide installation, consumption is denied as the image shifts between veiling and unveiling.

The veil continues to dominate Al-Ani's work, but as a metaphor for emotional candour and complex identity, rather than explicit cultural representation. Facets of each woman's personality have been gradually revealed, as Al-Ani has developed a long-term engagement with the group as the central motivating force and subject of her practice.

Eva Rueschmann's recent book on sisterly relationships in film reveals how post-1960s cinema has articulated the ways in which biological sisters negotiate mutuality and difference, co-author family histories, and profoundly shape each other's political and personal identities.[6] Rueschmann suggests the films of Margarethe von Trotta, Gillian Armstrong and Jane Campion, which typically feature female protagonists entangled in relations of intense emotional interdependence, display a complexity in their characters rarely seen in films which depict women solely in relation to their male counter-parts. Al-Ani's *1001 Nights* provides a clear example of how the artist allows characterisation between the women to build the work from anxious memory, through the horrifying and fantastical imagination, to curious contemplation, so that the mother and sisters come to act as facets of feminine subjectivity dealing with the personal and political through reoccurring dreams, and specifically as co-authors of their ongoing history.

Al-Ani's *Portraits*, a series of photographs shown alongside *A Loving Man* at the Imperial War Museum in 1999, depicts each woman, her hands clasped over her face as if caught between a howl of grief and a cry of joy. Their gestures seem poignantly reminiscent now of the surviving women of Beslan, though they could equally be read through the scope of melodramatic theatrical gesture. Though compelling as a response to the aftermath of war beyond the spectacle of disaster, it is perhaps *A Loving Man* that may be read as closest to Aristotle's original definition of tragedy.

Al-Ani's chorus of women relate the denouement of relationships with a 'loving man'. His act of *hamartia* was to make promises he couldn't keep. Her combination of interruption, repetition and shifts in tone and expression prevents the sentimentalising of the story. The single voice is fractured between mother and daughters, the relationships to the man remaining uncertain. The declaration 'I have freedom from the exile's gloom' banishes the threat that the women might be seen as victims, but even so they conclude broken-hearted. This work arouses empathy, compels through fragmented narrative, but perhaps most surprisingly engages through the anticipation of resolution. The story resides in the inevitability of their predicament of loss, in their and our hope for reconciliation or understanding. It is surely a work of ancient and contemporary tragedy.

1 Aristotle, *Poetics*, 350 BC (trans. Malcolm Heath), Penguin Classics, 2004
2 See Michael Billington, 'Terror of modern times sets the stage for Greek tragedy', *The Guardian*, June 19 2004
3 Slavoj Zizek, 'A Holiday from History', *dial H-I-S-T-O-R-Y*, Ofstfildern-Ruit, Hatje Cantz Publishing, 2004
4 Jean Fisher, 'Reflections on Echo – sound by women artists in Britain', *Signs of the Times: A Decade of Video, Film and Slide-Tape installation in Britain*, Museum of Modern Art, Oxford, 1990, p. 61
5 *Veil: Veiling, Representation and Contemporary Art*, published by inIVA in association with Modern Art Oxford to coincide with the touring exhibition *Veil*, co-curated by Al-Ani
6 *Sisters on Screen: Siblings in Contemporary Cinema*, Philadelphia, PA: Temple University Press, 2000

A Loving Man | Transcript

A loving man who broke my heart
He looked so young and optimistic once
He was my hero, he was loving and he made me laugh
He was in love and made promises he couldn't keep
I am my father's daughter in so many ways
I understood his dilemma
He never joined us, he tried but did he try hard enough?
Complete disbelief, frustration and deep anger
When politics, religion, war and cultures clash, it's the ordinary family that pays the price
He wrote to me of his anguish and loneliness and his memories of us as though we had all died
He feels deserted by us and we feel deserted by him
Regrets, my regrets, your regrets, his regrets
He's been a stranger to me for so long
There's no special person for me now
I can live my life more fully with him not near me
I have freedom from the exile's gloom
He is full of contradictions
Will he ever understand?
Will he ever love me for who I am?
He has broken my heart

She Said | Transcript

Sisters are so insistent
My sister writes to me and says...

Where shall I go?
How far back do I go?

Tell us how we started
So that's where we started

His family is not on the map
Things in our family were not talked about

I want to be the best I can
I want to be the first to tell you

Where are we now?
Where are we now?

Nobody helped us in time
Nobody actually listened to her

People hear what they want to
People say what they want to

It's really good to try something new
It was very good advice actually

She doesn't know what I'm talking about
He hasn't a clue what I'm talking about

Everything fits together now
Everything is censored

Why ask these questions?
I want you to ask me questions

It's all happening
They say they've done nothing

I must tell you something
I was telling you something

Did it go illegal at some stage?
This you may delete at some stage

What did they say?
What did you say?

We'll all help
What was it all about?

Who's going to feed us?
Who's going to be seeing this?

Nobody actually listened to her
I don't really listen to her

We don't need all this noise
I can't take the noise

1st woman
I wake up, it's the middle of the night and I'm in our house in Kirkuk. Outside, there's the sound of guns and bombs. I jump up. I realise my husband isn't there. I'm alone with our four children. I've got to get them out, I'm scared, mustn't panic. Quickly, get them up, they're very sleepy, walk them out, go towards the car. There are people running past, bombs exploding still, cars racing along. Safely, we're all now in the car. Then I remember, I don't know how to drive.

2nd woman
We're in Iraq, I can't remember what's happening, there's an event, and I'm thinking, it's strange to be back but it's nice. And then suddenly there's a declaration of war, and it's a real panic because people are all in different places. There are lots of taxis and cars going by. We're in a driveway, I think it's E2 — Amal and Eman's house. I'm in a taxi and I'm collecting everybody. I've collected, I think it might be Jananne and Nadia, and I'm looking for someone else, it might be Norah, I can't remember. Don't know who's missing and who's there. It's a real panic now, and everybody in the camp is in a panic and everybody's trying to leave but some people I think are hiding in their houses and decide to stay. I don't remember what happens in the end but there's this feeling of I don't believe this is happening. We should never have come back.

3rd woman
Everything's brown. There's been a war. You can hear the planes and the bombs. Everyone's been killed except two of us and we're wandering through the rubble and the buildings trying to hide from the soldiers. The brown uniforms and the brown guns with the bayonets. We keep having to dodge behind remnants of cars and buildings as the soldiers walk up and down the streets looking for people that are still alive. We see a scene in what's left of an old building, just dead bodies all over the floor and two soldiers using bayonets to spear the people to check that they are definitely dead. And just as I notice it, the girl that I'm with gets shot and falls to the floor. They haven't seen me yet, I'm still half hiding behind the building and I'm absolutely terrified, I know that I'm going to die but I still know that I've got to try and escape. So I try to creep away while they're checking if she's still alive or not and as I start to walk slowly I hear one of them shout and they turn around to me and I just run for my life. And then I hear a shot and just then I feel the bullet in my back, and I wake up, gasping.

4th woman
I look out of the bedroom window into the back garden, and beyond the garden is a fence. Beyond the fence there's some hills, and coming over the hills are hundreds of soldiers coming towards the house. We realise that we have to leave. So, we run out of the house and we get into the car which is still in the garage and just as the car is pulling out of the garage, we see this enormous rhinoceros coming round the side of the house and we realise that we're going to die.

5th woman
We're driving through the desert in a big black limousine. I'm in the car with my mother and three sisters. It's boiling outside but we've got huge heavy coats on and big boots. We suddenly come to a stop, our driver tells us to get out and start running. We run behind him. We can see two soldiers in the distance. Between them is a white line painted in the sand. On the other side of the white line is another black limousine and although the windows are blacked out, I know that our father is in that limousine. Our driver goes up to one of the soldiers and hands him all our paperwork. The soldier shakes his head and gives them back to our driver. The driver explains that they won't let us cross the line because one of our documents isn't in order, we're missing a piece of paper, we'll have to go back. I sit down on the side and I start to cry. The others start arguing with the driver. The soldier then starts to tell the other limousine to turn around and go and tells us to go back to our car. We all stand there and watch the limousine drive off into the distance.

Jananne Al-Ani

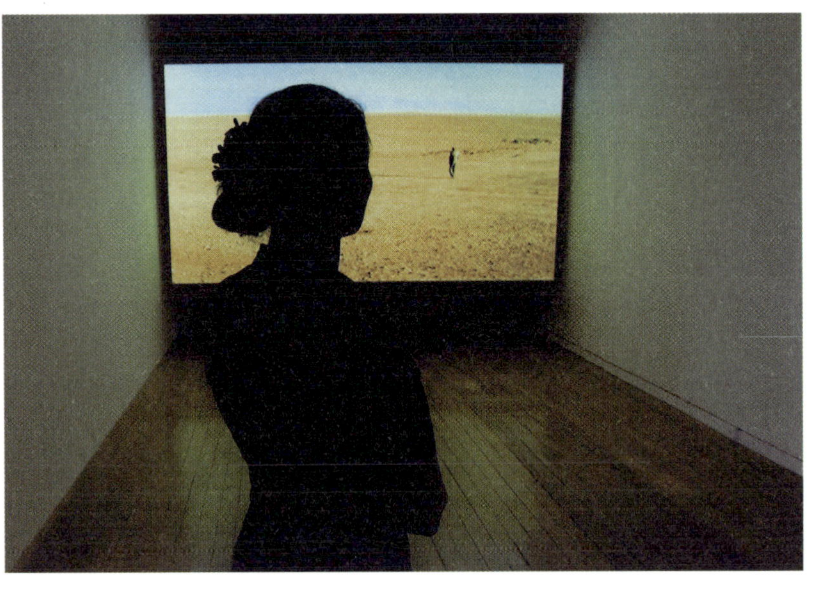

Muse (installation Norwich Gallery) | 2004 | Courtesy Eastern Daily Press

1966	Born in Kirkuk, Iraq
	Lives and works in London
1995/7	Royal College of Art
1986/9	Byam Shaw School of Art

Selected Solo Exhibitions

2005	*The Visit* Art Now, Tate Britain, London*
2004	*The Visit* Norwich Gallery
2002	Dryphoto Art Contemporanea, Toscana Fotografia 2002, Prato*
	Musée Reattu, Les Rencontres de la Photographie, Arles*
1999	Authur M Sackler Gallery, Smithsonian Institution, Washington DC
	Imperial War Museum, London
1998	Margaret Harvey Gallery, St Albans
1997	Harriet Green Gallery, London

Curated Exhibitions

2003/4	*Veil* The New Art Gallery Walsall – touring to Bluecoat Arts Centre; Open Eye Gallery, Liverpool; Modern Art Oxford and Kulturhuset Stockholm*
2001/2	*Fair Play* Danielle Arnaud Contemporary Art, London – touring to Angel Row Gallery, Nottingham*

Selected Group Exhibitions

2005	*The World is a Stage: Stories behind Pictures* Mori Art Museum, Tokyo
2004	*Amman Meeting Points* Al Beit, Amman
	Stranger Than Fiction: From the Arts Council Collection City Art Gallery, Leeds – touring to Tullie House Museum and Art Gallery, Carlisle; Aberystwyth Arts Centre; Usher Gallery, Lincoln; Nottingham Castle Museum and Brighton Museum and Art Gallery*
	Beyond East and West: Seven Transnational Artists Krannert Art Museum, Champaign, Illinois – touring to Louisiana State University Museum of Art, Baton Rouge, Louisiana; Hood Museum of Art, Dartmouth College, Hanover, New Hampshire and Williams College Museum of Art, Williamstown, Massachusetts*
2003	*The New Scheherazades* Centre de Cultura Contemporània de Barcelona – touring to Muséum d'Histoire Naturelle de Lyon*
	DisOrientation Haus der Kulturen der Welt, Berlin*
	And the One doesn't stir without the Other Ormeau Baths Gallery, Belfast*
	Love Affairs IFA-Galerie Stuttgart – touring to Bonn and Berlin*
	Alethia: the Real of Concealment Göteborgs Konstmuseum, Gothenburg*

2002 *Sans Commune Mesure: Image et Texte dans l'Art Actuel* Musée d'Art Moderne, Lille*
Fair Play: De nouvelles règles du jeu Fondation d'Art Contemporain Daniel et Florence Guerlain, Les Mesnuls*
Curio Hanbury Street, London*
Elsewhere WBD, Berlin
The John Kobal Photographic Portrait Award National Portrait Gallery, London*
Identinet web-based work commissioned by Film and Video Umbrella
2001 Essor Gallery, London
Tweener Norwich Gallery
EV+A 2001: Expanded Limerick City Gallery of Art*
2000 *Ekbatana?* Nikolaj Contemporary Art Centre, Copenhagen*
East International Norwich Gallery*
Strokes of Genius: Contemporary Iraqi Art Brunei Gallery, London*
Attitude: A History of Posing Victoria & Albert Museum, London
In Memoriam The New Art Gallery Walsall*
Look Out: Art Society Politics Wolverhampton Art Gallery – touring to Pitshanger Manor Gallery, London*
1998 *Shoreditch Biennale* London
On Site Lauderdale House, London
Photofit Bluecoat Gallery, Liverpool
1997 *Modern Narrative* Artsway, Sway*
20/20 Kingsgate Gallery, London*
1996 *Contemporary Art from the Collection* Imperial War Museum, London
After Eden an Ikon Gallery Project, Yoxall, Staffordshire
The John Kobal Photographic Portrait Award National Portrait Gallery, London – touring to The Royal Photographic Society, Bath; Scottish National Portrait Gallery, Edinburgh and Midland Art Centre, Birmingham*
1995 *Natural Settings* The Chelsea Physic Garden, London*
1994 *Who's Looking at the Family?* Barbican Art Gallery, London*
1993 *No More Heroes Anymore* The Royal Scottish Academy, Edinburgh
Declarations of War: Contemporary Art from the Collection of the Imperial War Museum Kettle's Yard, Cambridge
1992 *Fine Material for a Dream...? A Reappraisal of Orientalism* Harris Museum and Art Gallery, Preston – touring to Ferens Museum and Art Gallery, Hull and Oldham Art Gallery*
1991 *Contact: South Bank Photo Show* Royal Festival Hall, London*
Sign of the Times Camerawork, London
Guernica revisited Kufa Gallery, London
* Catalogue

Awards

2004 Arts Council England: Grants for the Arts
2003 London Artists Film and Video Development Award
2000/1 London Arts Board
2000 East International
1999 Artsadmin Bursary
1996 John Kobal Photographic Portrait Award

Public Collections

Arts Council England
Ferens Art Gallery, Hull
Imperial War Museum, London
Pompidou Centre, Paris
Smithsonian Institution, Washington DC
Victoria & Albert Museum, London

Selected Publications

2004 *Performing Difference* Rohini Malik Okon, Artsadmin
Transmission: Speaking & Listening (Volume 3) Sharon Kivland and Lesley Sanderson, Sheffield Hallam University/Site Gallery
Encyclopædia of the Modern Middle East and North Africa Philip Mattar, Thomson Gale
Beyond East and West: Seven Transnational Artists David O'Brien and David Prochaska, Krannert Art Museum
2003 *Veil: Veiling, Representation and Contemporary Art* Institute of International Visual Arts, in association with Modern Art Oxford
Home Works Christine Tohme and Mona Abu Rayyan, Ashkal Alwan: The Lebanese Association for Plastic Arts
2001 *Fair Play* David Barrett, Danielle Arnaud Contemporary Art
EV+A 2001: Expanded Salah Hassan and Paul M O'Reilly, Gandon Editions
Strokes of Genius: Contemporary Iraqi Art Maysaloun Faraj, Saqi Books
1998 *Beyond the Legacy* T Lawton and TW Lentz, Smithsonian Institution
1997 *Opening Lines* Alison Raftery, London Arts Board

Jananne Al-Ani would like to thank – Gill Addison, Sivine Ariss, Danielle Arnaud, Suzy Barnes, Suky Best, Richard Bonner-Morgan, Gilly Booth, Sylvie Borel, Juliette Brown, Rodrigo Cannas, Noel Chanan, Monica Chung, Lucinda Clark, Charlotte Cotton, Simon Crocker, Richard Crowe, Roland Denning, Claire Doherty, Lizzy Dyson, Sharon Essor, Alex Estrella, Maysaloun Faraj, Massumeh Farhad, Manick Govinda, Maja Grafe, Michael Guida, Mark Haworth Booth, Lynn Hewett, Richard Hylton, Alana Jelinek, Ann Jones, Frances Kearney, Michket Krifa, Jari Lager, Mary Lowthian, Simon Moretti, Faith Moore, Anoop Patel, Judy Price, Walid Raad, David Robinson, Deborah Robinson, Peter Sago, Jayce Salloum, Maureen Saunders, Timothy Saunders, Matthew Shaul, Maryrose Sinn, Roger Tatley, Christine Tohme, Nadine Touma, Christine van Assche, Bettina von Zwehl, Norah Walsh, Angela Weight, Carey Young and John Young

at Film and Video Umbrella – Steven Bode, Bevis Bowden, Nina Ernst, Lindsay Evans, Judith Glynne, Mike Jones, Caroline Smith and Keith Whittle

at Norwich Gallery – Gaynor Egan, Paul Kuzemczak, Lynda Morris, Thomas Salt, Neil Smallbone and Emma-Jayne Taylor

at Tate Britain – Ray Burns, Judith Nesbitt, Emily Pethick and Shuja Rahman

Jananne Al-Ani

Published by Film and Video Umbrella
Edited by Steven Bode
Editorial Assistance from Nina Ernst
Designed by Richard Bonner-Morgan
Printed by Trichrom Ltd

Publication supported by Arts Council England
with additional support from University of the Arts London, London College of Communication

Printed in an edition of 1,000
ISBN 1 90427 014 x

Published in conjunction with the touring exhibition, *The Visit* by Jananne Al-Ani, commissioned by Film and Video Umbrella and Norwich Gallery

The Visit
Cinematography – Noski Deville
First Assistant Camera – Peter Emery
Stills Photography – Effie Paleologou
Unit Driver/Production Assistant – Kamil Ahmed Ali
Ann, Nadia, Norah, Shatha and Subhi Al-Ani

Special thanks to – Wijdan Ali, Noor Al Qasimi, Raed Asfour, Maggie Ellis, Malu Halasa, Farhan Halasah, Azza Hammoudi, Serene Huleileh, Rose Issa, Joumana Kawar, Jack Persekian, Ra-ey Saleh and Gary Thomas

Film and Video Umbrella
52 Bermondsey Street London SE1 3UD
T 020 7407 7755 F 020 7407 7766
E info@fvu.co.uk W www.fvumbrella.com

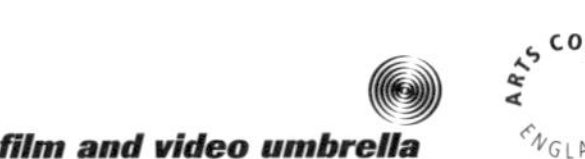

UNIVERSITY OF THE ARTS LONDON **LONDON COLLEGE OF COMMUNICATION** CAMBERWELL COLLEGE OF ARTS CENTRAL SAINT MARTINS COLLEGE OF ART AND DESIGN CHELSEA COLLEGE OF ART AND DESIGN LONDON COLLEGE OF FASHION